SURVIVING
HIGH-CONFLICT DIVORCE:

A Father's Story

Shane O'Brian

Mountain Page Press
HENDERSONVILLE, NC

Published 2021 by Mountain Page Press

ISBN 978-1-952714-03-0
Copyright © 2021 Shane O'Brian

All rights reserved.
No part of this publication may be reproduced, stored in a retrieval system, distributed or transmitted in any form or by any means (electronic, mechanical, photocopying, recording, or otherwise) without prior written permission from the publisher.

For information, contact the publisher at:
Mountain Page Press
118 5th Ave. W.
Hendersonville, NC 28792
Visit: www.mountainpagepress.com

This is a work of creative non-fiction. All of the events in this memoir are true to the best of the author's memory. Some names and identifying features have been changed to protect the identity of certain parties. The views expressed in this memoir are solely those of the author.

The author makes reasonable efforts to present accurate and reliable information in this book; The author is not responsible for any errors in or omissions references or websites listed or other information contained in this book, nor is the author responsible for the timeliness of the information contained on those websites or external references.

CONTENTS

Preface v

Surviving "I Want a Divorce" 1

Mediation and Anger 19

What You Need to Know: Am I Dealing with a Narcissist? 27

Finding a Lawyer 37

Bargaining: Trying to End the Insanity 49

Telling the Kids 53

Separating Space 63

My First Day in Court 71

Child Protective Services Custody Study 79

Child Support 89

And Then Came Panic Attacks 97

Evidence 107

Prayers Unanswered 119

Stealing Jennifer's Daughters 125

Dating and Filling the Void 133

Things Can Always Get Worse 143

Trial 147

The Last Hearing 163

The Final Divorce Decree 171

Finding Peace 177

Negotiating with K 181

Epilogue 185

Acknowledgements 187

PREFACE

All the noise of the outside world has suddenly stopped. The wars, famine, flooding, fires, politics, pandemics, and all the world's insanity no longer have any meaning for you. You are totally and completely enveloped in your small space on this planet, and, as everything you once knew is slipping away, you are left to the task of picking up the pieces—or just discarding everything. Thoughts of checking out are not far away.

If you're reading this, I can only imagine that you're in a world of hurt. Please know that I'm not a psychologist, lawyer, therapist, or mediator. I'm simply a guy who truly loves his kids and his family, one who went through a terrible high-conflict divorce from a narcissistic spouse who happened to have a sociopath for a boyfriend. I'll do my best to keep this real and informative.

I am writing this from first-hand experience. I'm writing for those people whose lives have been thrown into a tailspin—and it seems like there's no recovery. I'm writing because there are too many factors to make sense of why your spouse has asked you for a divorce. But you have come to this juncture. At this time you have to collect yourself, look at things as objectively and as calmly as possible, and move forward.

Everyone will have a different experience, but the emotions filling your days are feelings that many people can relate to—many more than you realize. I've put my experiences and insight into the following pages to help you get through this time in your life—a time that you may think no one in the world can understand.

SHANE O'BRIAN

This is a true story; it is accurate as far as sequence and circumstance is concerned, but all names and places have been changed in order to protect my children.

At the end of each chapter I offer suggestions based on what I found useful, and I have some strategies that might help with navigating the real challenges that are getting thrown at you.

It is my sincere hope that by reading this memoir you take away some sense of solace in knowing there are people who have experienced the tragedy of high-conflict divorce, and come out the other side, forever changed, but healthy and happy.

Amor Fati

CHAPTER ONE

SURVIVING "I WANT A DIVORCE"

In a single moment, your entire world changed.

I was either totally naïve or just too busy with the kids, work, and life to realize what was happening. I honestly didn't see it coming. Our marriage wasn't all sunshine and roses, but I in no way expected my wife of over twenty years to throw away everything—everything we had built together. Little did I know.

The day had started out great. The kids were home. It was summer break, and everything was normal. Then my wife Gigi arrived home from one of her extended layovers and turned a nice summer day upside down.

Gigi walked in the door, and it was apparent something was up. The house was clean and dinner was already in the works, but I guess it wasn't up to her standards. She glared at me as she rolled her suitcase through the living room. No warm hello, no kiss, no "How is your day going?" Just the stare of contempt.

My wife had been acting strange for a long time, and the kids and I were often walking on eggshells whenever she came in the door. That particular day Gigi seemed to be angrier than usual. She immediately started to berate our daughter about the house, the laundry, her room, her hair, and anything else she could think of. While I generally tried to stay out of the mother-daughter dynamic, this time I had to jump in to defend Elisha. There was no logical reason for my wife to be going so off-the-charts ballistic on a fifteen-year-old girl. I knew in that moment I had to do something. I got between Gigi and Elisha, and with my back to Elisha I held Gigi's hands and told her to stop. She became enraged at me as she struggled to get to our daughter.

"Shane, get the hell out of my way, I am not putting up with this bullshit. I've been gone for three days and come home to this little shit with an attitude. Now get out of my way."

If I didn't know better, I would have thought that Gigi had been drinking. I sent Elisha to her room and tried to defuse the situation.

Gigi did not like me taking the side of my daughter, so she turned on me. She went on an offensive rant, and what had been a nice peaceful day became, in an instant, a battle.

This scene had played out too many times over the previous year. And in that time, my flight-attendant wife had taken to flying as many layover flights as possible. She was gone about half the time. She told me that due to a change in the airline policy, she had to fly the layover flights. One of the many lies I had believed.

This new family dynamic of mom being gone half the time had taken some getting used to. I did my best to keep things normal in the house, and I thought we were a happy family.

However, something had changed with Gigi. I slowly became accustomed to the drama she created in the house and, for right or wrong, I tolerated it. It wasn't until—on this particular day—Gigi took to slapping my daughter that I knew I had to do something. I had to find out why she was always so mad and figure out how to move forward as a family. Our two sons, Daniel and John, were not usually in Gigi's crosshairs, but everyone in one way or another was feeling the tension, it was palpable. While I dreaded it, I knew it was time to have a heart-to-heart with Gigi.

The following day I asked her to take a drive with me. I didn't want things to blow up in the house with the kids at home. I drove to a nice area overlooking the ocean, parked, and took a deep breath. "I know you've been under a lot of stress. You are flying a lot, and I want to be a good husband for you, but you are making it impossible for all of us. You are always angry, and you seem to hate me, so can you tell me what the hell is going on?"

After some serious prodding, Gigi finally said something I completely did not expect. "Shane, I don't love you anymore and I want a divorce."

"What the hell are you talking about? I know things aren't perfect, but what in God's name are you saying?"

"I'm saying I don't love you anymore and I haven't loved you for a long time now. I want out."

"What is really going on here, Gigi? Is there someone else? Are you having an affair?"

"Fuck you, Shane! What is going on is that I don't love you."

My head was spinning, and I couldn't comprehend what I was hearing. I had just been stabbed in my heart, and I was at a loss as to why. Gigi would only say that she was no longer happy in our marriage and she wanted out. She didn't love me and hadn't loved me for some time. We had never even mentioned divorce to each other prior to this. It was as if my world had been ripped from my hands. Everything I thought I once knew—everything I was sure of—was suddenly gone . . . and I was empty.

We drove home together in silence. Gigi left the house to go get some "alone time," and I was left to be the parent. By myself. I put on my best face for the kids and tried to act as if nothing was wrong. Gigi didn't come home until very late that night. I was sitting in the living room as she came through the front door. She stared at me, and without a word, she walked down the hall to our bedroom. I heard her lock the door. About twenty minutes later, as I sat in disbelief on the couch, I heard her emerge from our room and go into the guest room, again locking the door behind her. I knew things were not going to get better anytime soon.

It was a few days after Gigi had told me she no longer loved me and wanted a divorce that I completely broke down. By then I was exhausted, as I had not truly slept for all that time. Gigi had been sleeping in the guest room. I walked down the hall and knocked on the guest room door to see if I could talk with her in a civil manner.

"We have to talk. I really think I deserve some answers. Please come to bed."

She reluctantly agreed. My life and my future were about to be irreversibly changed, and the thought of losing my family simply put me over the edge. My emotions spilled out and I began to cry. .

Up to that point, Gigi had insisted that there was no one else, and she had simply fallen out of love—but I knew in my heart that was not the case.

"Who is he? Tell me who he is. There must be someone else, so tell me his name. Who is he, Gigi?"

It was probably thirty minutes of back and forth, her anger growing toward the man who loved her, before she finally gave up a name.

"His name is Jason; we're in love, and I can't stay with you any longer."

"Is he your co-worker? Is he married?" My mind spinning, I felt sick to my stomach. "Does he have kids?"

"He's a pilot and he is going through a divorce. That is all you need to know! I can't stand being around you—and that is what you'd better understand!"

She seemed so cold. It's almost as if I had never met her. "How many kids does he have?"

"He has two daughters, which has nothing to do with this!"

"What's his wife's name?"

Gigi was getting very impatient with me, but I was not going to let this go. She was having an affair and had betrayed my children and me. I wanted answers.

"Why the hell do you want to know that?"

"Because now I have to keep her and her kids in my prayers."

"Shane, you are such an asshole!"

"What's her name? Tell me her name."

"Her name is Jennifer, she lives in Georgia with her daughters. This conversation is over, I want a divorce!"

I couldn't get the thought of my kids out of my mind. They were going to be devastated, and I had to try to fight for our family—even through all this ugliness. I tried another tack.

"Babe, I love you. What about our kids? Are you thinking of them at all?"

"Shut the fuck up, Shane. I love the kids more than anything. They are my kids, and they will understand this shit; so stop acting like this isn't your fault!"

It was my first taste of the evil that was my wife. Her complete lack of empathy for our children and me—it freaked me out.

While everyone's story is unique, you may be facing a divorce—or the fallout of a divorce. Realize that you're not alone, and many people have gone through something similar.

When your world is collapsing around you and you don't know if you can make it through the day, let alone the week, the month, or the year, finding the strength to be at peace—to find any sense of calm—can feel impossible. It's at this time, when everything seems to be going against you, that you must stop and look at what's good in your life—the things that make you want to keep living. Embrace those things and do not lose sight of them. Think of friends, family, love of life, and understand that you're far better off than so many less fortunate souls. Whether it is the sunrise, the dew on the grass, children playing with their dog in the park, a rainbow, beautiful flowers, or an orange sunset—whatever makes you smile, keep that in mind. Know that the world is still a magnificent place with more beauty than you can ever behold. Life is great, and this is a blip in time.

First Step

After the surreal exchange with Gigi, my sense of worth was destroyed. It seemed like an eternity before I felt that I could reach out for help. I was profoundly embarrassed, and telling anyone seemed beyond me. After a couple weeks keeping everything bottled up inside, I finally came to the point that I could tell someone my story, so I turned to an attorney friend I've known since the early 90s. Sam gave me some powerful advice.

"Shane, you have to try marriage counseling. For the kids' sake you have to try."

"It's not that easy, Sam. Gigi is sleeping with a married pilot. How the hell am I supposed to overlook that shit?"

"Listen, I've seen this a thousand times. It's the kids who suffer the most. If you love them, you have to give it a shot."

The feeling of being betrayed—and having my children betrayed—was overwhelming, so counseling was not an easy decision; but I did it. I looked in the phone book and found a family psychologist and made the appointment.

I struggled getting the nerve up to ask, but I knew if I were to save my family I had to try. I let Gigi know I had scheduled an appointment with a marriage counselor, Dr. Faith Ross. I actually had to invoke the children's names to get Gigi to agree to go. We went to the first session, where Dr. Faith greeted us warmly. Gigi sat as far away from me as physically possible. I felt like a disease. The therapist asked for the basic rundown of what was happening, and I set out the whole story.

Surviving "I want a Divorce"

I think that when Gigi heard the scenario spoken aloud to a stranger, it sent a shock wave through her. Sitting there on that couch, she looked like a spoiled child who had just been scolded for the first time in her life. If looks could kill, Dr. Faith and I would have both been dead. The session ended with no progress. As we walked out of the clinic, I could feel the hate pouring out toward me.

"What a fucking waste of time Shane, you're an idiot."

In hindsight, I should have realized that my wife had already made her decision. I begged her to go to one more session—and she did—but we made no progress. Truthfully, Gigi wasn't willing to even speak to Dr. Faith, and by the end of that session the psychologist's statement was clear.

"I cannot help you two as a couple. If one of you wants to continue counseling, I am happy to see one of you, but I can't see you both unless you are both willing to move forward together."

I told Dr. Faith that I did want to continue therapy. Gigi, on the other hand, had no interest in marriage counseling or therapy for herself.

It was soon after our second attempt at marriage counseling that Gigi stopped coming home. She told me that she was going to be staying with a friend, but it didn't take a brain surgeon to figure out exactly where she was. My kids were accustomed to mom being gone for extended periods of time, so when she packed a suitcase and walked out the door, they thought nothing of it. *Mom's just going on another trip.*

With Gigi's refusal to take part, counseling wasn't an option for our marriage. That's not to say it isn't an option for yours. If you can get past the hate and rejection you feel, try counseling. If for no other reason, you can attempt to open up a channel of communication.

If you have kids, for their sake, try to work things out. A trained psychologist or therapist will educate you on how to deal with this huge life event with your children foremost in your thoughts and actions.

Divorce is a wound on a child that may never heal. Until you or your spouse is dead and buried, your children—even after they become adults—will likely hope and pray that, against all odds, "Mom and Dad will get back together, and we will be a family again." I realize this may not be true for everyone, but my marriage was not a scream-fest. For many years, ours was the picture-perfect family life. I'm sure my children will miss that forever.

The Why

Along with seeking help, try to understand why this is happening. Something has gone terribly wrong with your relationship, so be honest with yourself. Take the time to contemplate the issues that have led to this point. For me, writing out my thoughts and feelings helped me understand them better. When you write things down, they become clearer. Make a list of why you may consider staying in the marriage and another list of why it's best to part ways—and then wait. That's right. Wait. Your emotions at this stressful time may run incredibly hot. You want things to be done—you want it to be over, but if you set things aside, they'll tend to look very different the next day, so take your time.

Whenever you're hit with a tragic life event like a death in a family, or in this case the death of a family, you'll go through an emotional cycle. The psychology books and blogs all pretty much say the same thing; there are 5 stages to grieving the end of life—or that of a relationship (the Kübler-Ross model). The stages are denial, anger, bargaining, depression, and acceptance.

Denial (Stage 1)

The first stage when you're dealing with a tragic and unforeseen event is denial.

Surviving "I want a Divorce"

This can't be happening to me! I'm a good person. I don't deserve this! She'll come to her senses and this will all go away.

When the person you considered your best friend and lifelong companion is suddenly saying she wants out, it's devastating.

This happens to other people, not to me.

This might be hard to accept, but it's exactly what I read over and over as I went through pages and pages of literature regarding this subject. People grow apart. You may have been in this relationship for years. You and your spouse are not the same people who walked down the aisle together. Life experiences have changed you and they've changed your partner.

In a perfect world your experiences bring you closer together. In a perfect world you and your spouse would have stayed in shape and kept the sex life lively and fun. You wouldn't have lost hair in some places and grown it in others. You'd both have held the same vision for the future, common goals, common beliefs, and common priorities; and when you had a problem, you would have worked things out in a way that brought you closer.

But we do not live in a perfect world—and many issues can derail a marriage. Of course, a wandering eye and infidelity is one of the most common factors in divorce. Whatever the reason, try to understand it—and understand that it's not your fault. You are not to blame. Shit happens; and more than that, shit happens to everyone. No one escapes shit. It doesn't make this any easier, but it is a fact of life. Try to accept it.

Seeking Help

You're going to need help getting through this dark time. At first I was so embarrassed I couldn't bring myself to talk to anyone. I didn't want to tell my family. I didn't want to tell my friends. I wasn't part of a church and didn't have a trusted clergy member to turn to. I was very much alone.

It took weeks, but I eventually did tell my friends, then went on to tell my family. I was devastated at that time. I cried a lot. I was ashamed of myself. I was sure that everyone must have been thinking, *What is wrong with Shane that Gigi would dump him like that?*

The fact is, the more I spoke to people, the more clearly I was able to think. I had always been a spiritual person and I took to talking to God a lot more. I gave going to church a try.

God and any trusted person are great choices to lean on for support. If you're anything like me, you're normally the one who gets leaned on and doesn't do any leaning. But at a time like this, learn to take advantage of the relationships you have with family and loved ones. There's no shame in talking about your emotions and venting about the divorce and how it makes you feel, how angry you are, and how this is affecting your children. These are things you must get out of your system. Let them out.

Friends and family are great, but I hope you will consider seeking out an impartial professional to talk with. I do not live in a large city so going to a therapist is still very stigmatized in the small community where I live. I was lucky enough to find Dr. Faith, for which I am eternally grateful. Through my therapy with her I eventually found a sense of calm and was able to find the faith in myself to get through another week, another day, another minute.

If you belong to a church, I hope you'll go talk with the pastor or his wife, a priest, or an elder in your congregation. I guarantee they've had countless people approach them with this very same problem. Help is out there for you. There are online support groups for both men and women, and many universities offer free counseling. However you do it—do it! Get the help you need to work out the very confusing emotions. My sessions with Dr. Faith saved my sanity.

Seeking the Truth

It was after our failed attempt at marriage counseling that I started to seek answers about Gigi's affair and her new love. I have a few friends who are pilots, so I asked one of them to meet. He happened to fly for the same airline as Gigi. I simply told him I had something I wanted to discuss, and we met at one of the local hot spots for lunch. I arrived a bit early and was on my second beer by the time he arrived.

As a real estate broker, I had handled all of Steve's real estate needs for many years and we had always had a friendly relationship.

"Brother Steve, good seeing you man, how's life?"

"All good, Shane, how 'bout you? Looks like you've lost weight."

"Been a little stressed lately."

We took care of all the small talk over burgers and beers, and then I summoned the courage to bust out the real reason for the meeting.

"Steve, I need to ask you something and would appreciate you keeping everything confidential."

"You know it, Shane, what's going on?"

"Gigi is having an affair with a pilot. His name is Jason, but I don't know his last name. What can you tell me about him?"

"Shane, there's only one Jason in this base, and I am sure it couldn't be him. The dude is a bit of a religious fanatic. I can't stand flying with him because he'll quote Scripture from here to Japan and back. Must be someone from a different airline."

"His wife's name is Jennifer. Does that help?"

"Shit man, then it must be Jason Snider. I've met his wife Jen on a couple of flights when she was taking her kids on vacation. Wow, Shane, I'm really sorry."

Steve went on to tell me everything he knew about Jason, which was not a lot. He was not a well-liked co-pilot because he pushed his religious beliefs on the entire flight crew on every flight. Steve said he was more or less a pompous jerk. I thanked Steve for the information, and he assured me that he'd keep everything to himself. If word got out to any of the flight attendants, the rumor mill that is the airline industry would explode.

A True Godsend

There was one other person who came into my life at the beginning of my ordeal. She came at a time of utter despair, and I honestly thought she was a Godsend. It was about 2:00 AM. I had been up all night trying to make sense of things. Gigi had left with her boyfriend on a trip, leaving the kids and me to feel abandoned. I was a complete train wreck. And then the phone rang.

Wondering who could possibly be calling me at this hour, I answered the house phone (which almost never rang).

The lady on the other end asked, "Is this Shane?"

"Yes, it is."

"I have something to tell you."

Immediately, I guessed, "Is this Jennifer?"

It was Jason's wife. She seemed taken aback that I knew her name. It had been weeks since Gigi told me her name, but I had prayed for her and her kids every day, so the name Jennifer was embedded in my brain already.

"Yes, this is Jennifer. I want to let you know that your wife is having an affair with my husband."

Jennifer and I spoke for hours. I don't think I was what she expected. For whatever reason, we both shared a sense of guilt for the way our spouses were acting and the fact that their affair was having detrimental effects on five innocent souls: her two daughters and my three kids.

That phone call from Jennifer brought a little peace into my upside-down world. I told Jennifer that Gigi had told me her husband,

Surviving "I want a Divorce"

Jason, had asked her for a divorce. The story was either an outright lie from Gigi, or Jason had lied to her and she believed him. In either case, Jennifer let me know, to that point, Jason had not asked her for a divorce.

She had suspected the affair for many months, but only recently had she been able to confirm her suspicions. It was then that she decided to separate from Jason, not return to her home in my area, and to stay in Georgia with her daughters. She and the girls moved in with her parents.

During my discussion with Jennifer, it became very clear that the timeline of when Gigi told me she no longer wanted to be married was only a day or two after Jennifer told her husband that she was moving back to Georgia and wanted to separate. This was the third time Jennifer had discovered her husband's infidelity. I guess she had a three-strike rule.

In the weeks and months to come, I got to know Jennifer better. It seems strange to say, but a friendship blossomed, and to this day I speak with her often. I had found a person going through the exact same thing as I was at the exact same time. The ins and outs of our friendship could fill volumes, but that's not what this book is about.

Now, get ready. I realize this next bit of advice I am offering will be highly controversial and many people will disagree with it. This is based solely on my personal experience. I have done no research on the subject, but it worked for me.

If you're in the situation I was—your spouse having an affair with another married person—talk to that adulterer's spouse. The inside information I got from Jennifer saved my sanity and proved to be invaluable. Many times I knew more about Gigi's boyfriend than she did. Weird!

If you do plan to approach this person, do so cautiously and with no expectations. The spouse may not even know an affair is going on, so the response could be anger or complete denial. I don't want you to get into a conversation that may end terribly; so plan on what you would like to say, then keep it simple, direct, and most of all compassionate.

My life had just been thrown into a blender and turned on liquefy. I couldn't believe what was going on, and almost every person I told had the same reaction when I broke the news to them.

"No fucking way Shane! Is Gigi on drugs?"

To anyone looking in, we had the perfect life and the perfect relationship. We had money, three beautiful kids, wonderful vacations, and had a nice home. I was a dedicated father and husband, and no one saw this coming—especially me.

I want to add a bit of information about my marriage and the time leading up to my divorce. Gigi asked me for a divorce a few months prior to our twenty-first wedding anniversary. The year leading into the marriage collapse, we'd been planning a big move. The kids were getting older and we felt it was time to move. Gigi had plenty of seniority in the airlines and could transfer to another base, and I felt I could do real estate anywhere. We searched many communities in the U.S. and, as a family, decided on a home just outside Portland in a nice town called Cedar Mill. We signed the purchase agreement and put the down payment on a beautiful new home. With the children in tow, we visited the schools they would be attending and looked at the community, talked with neighbors, visited parks, and even shopped at stores in the area. I looked at the job market and interviewed with a couple real estate agencies. I took the opportunity to stop by the state-licensing bureau to pick up the paperwork and info on becoming licensed as an agent in Oregon. It was everything you'd do when you're about to make the move of a lifetime.

At this same time we put our home and an investment property on the market and soon had them both under contract of sale. I had already scheduled a moving company to pack us up and move us. I was a successful real estate broker and essentially gave away all my clients, referring them to other agent friends. We were just months away from moving and starting a new life together—as a family. When I packaged this all together, then added in, *Hey, my wife is having an affair, doesn't love me, and wants a divorce*, it was an avalanche. That's how it felt, like an avalanche crashing down on my children and me.

Getting through the Dark Times

I've already told you some of the things that I did to get me through the dark times. I spoke with friends and family, and I saw Dr. Faith once or twice a week. However, there's a lot more to it.

I'm going to go over this in later chapters; but after deep consideration, I think this is one of the most important things for you to internalize. It was for me. Remain calm. It's something that may save you from falling into the trap. You know—the trap of posting something stupid on social media or doing something provocative in public. You may feel compelled to take an ax to your spouse or their lover. Don't do it. Stay away from them as much as possible. Maintain your composure so there's no question about your being the good guy—and never resort to violence or anything else that will make you look like a danger to anyone. Keep your children close to your heart and stay calm.

Take Your Time

The one thing that dawned on me early in my journey through divorce was that things always look different if you just wait a day. Things tend to not be as bad as they first appear. When you wake up the next morning, you may see that, by not reacting—or more importantly, by not *overreacting*—you can keep some semblance of peace. You may have cried yourself to sleep the night before, but when you wake up, you'll be glad you protected your reputation and your children. Keep in mind that everyone is walking around with a camera, and anything that is said on social media is forever. If you confront your spouse or their paramour in public, it will likely be recorded and, in turn, be shown to your children or the police. Don't blow it by letting your anger get the best of you. Be the person your children know you to be: Dad.

Exercise

I was lucky in that I've always maintained a workout routine. Exercise helps to get that negative energy out of you while your body produces endorphins that help your brain cope. You'll burn excess energy and sleep better. If you've never had an exercise regiment, starting one during a divorce may be difficult, but I cannot stress enough the benefits you'll gain. You don't have to head to the gym; just get out there and take a brisk walk three or four days a week. If you live in an area with green space, walk in the woods or walk on the beach and get close to nature. You'll be a thousand miles ahead if you heed this one bit of advice; so for your sake and the sake of your children, get off your butt, get off your phone, and do something healthy. The other benefits are meeting people and looking better, which will help you gain confidence. Get up and do it.

A Positive Message

Listen to uplifting music. Whatever it is you like, listen to that music. I loved listening to old rock and roll, new rock and roll, classical music, Mozart, I even listened to some gospel and Christian music. Anything with a positive message is what you need to listen to. I remember listening to "Promises" by Clapton (not exactly uplifting but appropriate) and "Amazing" by Aerosmith over and over.

"It's amazing, when the moment arrives that you know you'll be alright."

Surviving "I want a Divorce"

A lot of insightful books are out there, so set aside some quiet time and read. In doing some intentional reading, I educated myself. I read books about helping my children through divorce I read uplifting books by Joel Osteen and Dr. Wayne Dyer. Not all the books I chose were therapeutic in nature; some old favorites were simply a means of escape from the ugliness. For example, during my cardio workouts I re-read some of my favorite books. It was an escape. The time would pass quickly, and I'd walk away sweaty and exhausted, but clear in my mind. Of course, the tragedy of the end of my family always came back into my consciousness and my world, but escaping for a bit gave my brain the rest it needed.

If reading isn't your thing, audio-books—along with podcasts and videos—with positive messages are available in abundance. If you go online, try watching some of the amazing stories and speeches on Goalcast. Try to take the messages to heart.

Overall, I guess I'm saying it's a good idea to keep yourself well rounded. This isn't the end of your life, but a new beginning. Even if you didn't want a new beginning, you got one; so make the best of it. Keep moving forward and remember: You're going through it; you are not stuck in it. Time heals.

When one door of happiness closes, another opens; but often we look so long at the closed door that we do not see the one which has been opened for us. —Helen Keller

Chapter One

Takeaways and Action Items

- When confronted with divorce, try to remain calm.

- Reach out for help and attempt marriage counseling.

- Write things down to try to understand why your marriage is in trouble. Remember that there are two of you, and you played a part in the trouble.

- The first emotion you will face is denial. Understand that it is normal to feel denial.

- Give it a day. Before reacting to something your spouse is doing or has done, give it one day before you react. Things look different in the morning.

- Find friends to talk to. Avoid putting anything on social media. Remember that anything you write can show up in court.

- Surround yourself with uplifting and positive messages in music, podcasts, or inspirational videos and stories. These messages might come from a faith tradition or a favorite ball team. It's a rough time, so find something good to focus on.

- Exercise and meditate. Burn off extra energy and learn to slow your mind. These practices will go a long way toward finding peace.

CHAPTER TWO

MEDIATION AND ANGER

The choice is this: Are you going to allow your anger to get the best of you, or will you think rationally and forego the war?

At all costs, avoid the war! If you can stay civil and work things through without a never-ending fight, that is what you should do. You may feel rage and hate toward your unfaithful partner, but in the end, take the necessary steps to keep your sanity, dignity, and sense of fair play intact. There is an old saying, "The only people who win in divorce are the lawyers." There has never been a truer statement.

The area where I live requires that if you file for divorce, you must try mediation. Ask your attorney or go online and find out the requirements in your jurisdiction.

Going through the process of mediation with your spouse creates the chance for a win for everyone. You will not get everything you want, but for your kid's sake, please be reasonable and participate to the best of your ability. Realize that material things really don't matter. When you're on your deathbed—which we all eventually will be—we won't care who got the car, or the silverware, or the house, for that matter. You'll care only about the impact you've had on others, especially your children.

After getting some sound advice from a friend, I set my sights on mediation. It was the beginning of the process, and although we'd gone nowhere with the marriage counseling, I thought this would be different. Seeing the psychologist was an attempt to keep my family together; mediation was an attempt to end the marriage in a civil manner, save on the legal fees, and—hopefully—have some thread of a family left intact.

Finding a Mediator

There were only two licensed mediation companies in my community, so I followed the advice of my attorney friend and set up a meeting with the one he recommended. I went to their office and spoke with the office manager. The wounds were still fresh, so telling my story to a stranger was extremely difficult. I have three kids and I knew that the divorce was going to tear them apart.

The mediation company will ask for a breakdown of the issues, where you stand, and how you think you would like to resolve the conflict. As I told the woman about my situation, I often had to pause and collect myself as I gave the details of my marriage and my unfaithful wife. I was literally brought to tears in front of this complete stranger. Not easy. But I got through it, and so will you.

After my meeting, I told Gigi that I'd made a mediation appointment and wanted to try this route before spending thousands on attorney fees. With that, I asked her to go in and fill out the paperwork and tell her side of the story. One session of mediation was $300, regardless of how long it lasted. I thought it was a reasonable price but still asked Gigi to pay half. It was the beginning of the end, and it seemed best to start moving in the direction of splitting things up. Gigi begrudgingly agreed to it.

Mediation and Anger

The time leading up to mediation day was hectic and trying. Every day held multiple challenges, and it was all I could do to get through in one piece. It felt overwhelming—I was attempting to cancel the sale contracts for the two homes we were selling as well as the new home we were buying in Portland. Those dreams were done. It was rough, but I kept on moving forward, one step at a time.

I'd like to say that I was patient and allowed things to happen in due time—but that would be a lie. The plan to move to Oregon made everything exponentially more difficult. I was facing the prospect of getting my real estate clientele back, canceling contracts to purchase and sell homes, getting the kids re-enrolled in the schools we had already told they would no longer be attending . . . there was just so much to do, and I wanted to get everything over with. The day for mediation—and a chance to start the end—could not have come quickly enough.

Mediation Day

The mediator was a charming retired judge. He was in his seventies and likely closing in on eighty. He was very well dressed for our casual small town atmosphere. His speech was clear and concise, and he was quick to smile. He introduced himself as Judge Stanford, gave us the rules of play, and asked that we respect them. He let us both know that, if needed, we could adjourn to separate rooms and he would speak with us individually.

Judge Stanford had already reviewed our statements and had a basic grasp of our precarious situation. He knew from experience that the main issues to be resolved were the kids and the finances. Custody is usually the most contentious issue in all divorces, so that's where we started. Since Gigi was already living with a married man, I pointed out that it was impossible to expect the kids to stay with her and her married boyfriend. The fact she was a flight attendant and away from home half the time was also a sticking point for me. These were obvious facts, and as in the case of Dr. Faith, hearing the issues spoken aloud with a stranger in the room made Gigi very uncomfortable. Even so, she remained adamant about the kids meeting her paramour as soon as possible.

At one point, the mediator stopped us and said, "Ma'am I'm not supposed to give advice, but you have to realize your situation and take into account your children's welfare. A judge will have a hard time granting you custody while you are living with a married man."

In that instance, Gigi looked like a goldfish—her mouth gaping open. She seemed at a loss for words but appeared to reluctantly accept the mediator's point.

As the session continued, we seemed to make some progress, but it was uncertain at best. Every new issue was a battle.

During that first session I had to sit across from Gigi. There she sat, the look of utter disdain in her eyes. The person I thought I knew better than anyone literally seemed to hate the sight of me. I felt lonely in my soul.

We'd been at it for a couple hours when the mediator said, "I think it's best we take a time-out, gather our thoughts, and come back in a couple days ready to resolve the issues involving the children. Then we can begin talking about the family finances and splitting assets."

We set the appointment, and I was cautiously optimistic. I knew I had an uphill battle, but I was willing to put in the work to avoid the high cost of a war.

My optimism was misplaced. Gigi cancelled the next session to go with her boyfriend on a trip to somewhere in Asia. She cancelled last minute, so we were on the hook for the $300 prepayment. We rescheduled and I grew more impatient by the minute.

A week later we were again set to meet with the mediator. Gigi showed up, but things had changed. She apparently had received advice from her boyfriend or her family and she came to the table with

Mediation and Anger

a defiant attitude. The negotiations went south. Fast. All the progress from our first session was lost. She had the Samuel L. Jackson look on her face that screamed, *"Fuck you, motherfucker."*

Judge Stanford did his best to keep things moving. We kept at it, but made little headway, as if digging a grave with a spoon. Although to me it seemed like an impossible feat, the mediator persisted. After an hour or so, he again said, "We need to take a break, gather our thoughts, and come back in a few days."

Gigi agreed to another session, which she cancelled, rescheduled, then cancelled again.

The mediation company manager was growing impatient with the constant rescheduling for Mrs. O'Brian. In my community the mediators are volunteers and do not get paid for their time, so I understood their frustration. But I could do nothing to force Gigi to be respectful. It was after the fourth cancellation that I knew it was time to move on and retain an attorney and prepare for what the legal system would bring.

I was not yet aware of what I was dealing with. I learned later that, in the case of divorcing a narcissist, mediation is truly not an option. One of the tell-tale signs that your spouse is a narcissist is their inability to negotiate.

My journey with the mediation company didn't end there. More on that later.

Though mediation didn't work for me, the good news is that roughly ninety-five percent of all divorces end in a settlement. Only five percent actually go to trial. My point is that you and your soon-to-be ex will, in all likelihood, end up settling. You're not going to get everything you want, and neither is your spouse. No matter who did what to whom, you're going your separate ways. If you don't have children, consider yourself very lucky. If you do have children, realize that, for better or worse, you'll be dealing with your kids' other parent for a long time. On some level, you will likely deal with them forever.

Anger (Stage 2)

"No good, goddamn jerk! This crap would be a lot easier if the idiot had just died."

How you deal with your anger can have serious ramifications on the outcome of the bitter journey of divorce. Although I felt betrayed by my ex and I fantasized about her demise, what really scared my family and friends was what I wanted to do to Gigi's boyfriend. I had heard countless stories of pilots fooling around with flight attendants. It permeates the airline industry. Fantasizing about the demise of your partner and their new best friend is totally normal. Please understand that acting on it will not end well for anyone. Including you.

Angry or not, I had to be there for my kids. I knew that if I did something stupid, I would end up in jail and would lose the most important part of my life, my three angels. I hope for your sake that you have the same amount of love for your kids as I have for mine. Forego the violence—and even the thought of violence—and simply realize that you're better off without your ex in your life. Whether you believe in fate or faith, there really is a plan for you.

My firm belief in karma really helped me. I knew that negative thoughts and negative energy would only end up hurting me. Even thinking about or wishing for Gigi's death was wrong. Wishing bad things to happen to anyone will mess up your karma. Hoping for bad things to happen to someone else—or actually making them happen—will eventually boomerang on you. Let your anger out. If that means an hour on the punching bag, or a hard run, or just screaming into a paper bag, let it out. At the end of the day, let that shit go and realize how amazingly lucky you are to be alive. Don't let the anger get to you. Don't dwell on it. Push it aside. It will only keep you down and never let you up; so move beyond it, then get up and smile.

Divorce changes your life, and you'll be better off the minute you accept that fact and take the steps to make the best of it. If something

Mediation and Anger

really pisses you off, remember: Do not act on it. Wait. Give it a day, and whatever it was that made you so angry won't be so bad the next morning. It may still be really messed up, but it won't be something you will want to kill over. Take the time to cool off. Nothing is worth your going to jail or losing your kids—nothing. Take a few deep breaths then ask God for peace and keep living.

This quote has been attributed to a Buddhist monk and I think it's right on:

Holding on to anger is like grasping a hot coal with the intent of throwing it at someone else; you are the one who gets burned.
—Buddhaghosa

Chapter Two

Takeaways and Action Items

- Do everything possible to avoid going to war with your spouse.

- Make the effort to mediate in good faith with your soon-to-be-ex spouse.

- Remember that 95% of all divorces end in some kind of settlement. Be reasonable.

- The second stage of grief is anger. It is normal to be angry.

- It is ok to feel anger. It is never ok to be violent.

- Keep your children in mind at all times. Stay focused on loving and keeping them.

- Let your anger out by seeking help from friends, family, and a professional. Letting it out is healthy.

- Let go of the negative thoughts and emotions as soon as you can. They will only tear you down. Remember to maintain exercise and meditation practices.

CHAPTER THREE

WHAT YOU NEED TO KNOW: AM I DEALING WITH A NARCISSIST?

*Who are you? I really want to know. Who the hell are you?
Is Gigi still in there anywhere, because I would like to talk to
her for a minute.*

I remember saying those exact words to the person I had lived with for over two decades. I was scared of what she had become. I was scared of what she would do next.

If your divorce has started out with no semblance of sanity, and if you don't recognize the person you are divorcing because they have changed to the umpteenth degree, then this chapter is for you. In my case, Gigi no longer spoke the same way. Her demeanor and the way she expressed herself—in her language and her body language—was completely different from the Gigi of the past twenty years. She became an entirely different person—one I did not know.

The biggest mistake I made in my divorce is that I didn't recognize my wife had a serious personality disorder. Narcissistic Personality Disorder (NPD) is real, and if your spouse has NPD then your journey through divorce will be long and arduous. I think the majority of the population does not understand NPD; and unless you experience it firsthand, Narcissus is just a character in Greek mythology.

After over twenty years of marriage, I thought if anyone knew Gigi, it was me. I thought I knew her strengths and weaknesses, her dreams and her vision for our children and our future. I thought I knew her morality. How could I not know this shit, right? How could I not know that the person I'd slept with for almost half my life had a serious personality disorder? What kind of moron can't see that his wife is a full-blown narcissist? Well, here I am. I had no idea who I was divorcing.

When I looked into Gigi's eyes as I spoke to her, I knew it was no longer the Gigi I knew who was looking back at me. It was a dead glare filled with anger and abhorrence. I could see in her eyes that she would prefer that I was no longer breathing. I've heard the term *narcissistic rage*, and that pretty well sums it up.

Narcissist: (N) A person who has an excessive interest in or admiration of themselves.

Characteristics of a narcissist: inflated self-image, arrogant, manipulative, selfish, patronizing, with a lack of empathy and consideration of others.

Narcissists can appear to be normal and may be successful in their careers but will fly off the handle when confronted with any kind of criticism.

During our marriage I knew that Gigi was selfish. I knew she cared deeply for the spotlight and always wanted to stand in it, alight in the glow. She would crave a new car or another glamorous handbag that she could wave in front of her friends' faces. When she would fixate on a new fashion or type of shoe, she would *need* every color and variation of that stretch pant or stiletto heel. The cost of things meant very little to her, and to say she was wasteful with money would be a significant understatement.

What You Need to Know: Am I Dealing with a Narcissist?

I could not keep Gigi from her impulse buying. She hated to be told anything and would always be quick to point out that she worked, and it was *her* money. When Gigi would bring home another bag that looked exactly like the other two that were sitting in the closet, I would protest; but money wasn't too important to me. Having a nice home and being able to send the kids to a good school was all I cared about, so I would usually look the other way and let it go. After all, as they say, "Happy wife, happy life."

One other thing I'll point out is that during our marriage I was a devoted and loving husband and father. Despite Gigi's shortcomings, I did love her, and I showed her my affection every day. There was not a day that went by that I did not tell her she was beautiful, and I was always quick to say I loved her. I didn't realize it, but it all fed into her need for narcissistic supply. I was feeding her need for attention and admiration. The fact that I would back down from an argument in order to keep the peace in the house was also giving her a sense of superiority and control.

Gigi's affair with a married man was a bridge too far for me. I let her know in no uncertain terms how truly fucked up a person she was to do that to our family. That was when the proverbial shit hit the fan.

Because I was suddenly no longer a source of positive energy for her, she sought to make me a source of negative energy. A narcissist feeds on both, and once they make that turn, you can expect your spouse to sink to new lows—just to make you miserable. Gigi would go to any depth to hurt me.

Using the Children as a Weapon

The most sickening part of all is that narcissists don't care if their children are collateral damage. As long as you are hurt, anyone else who may also be hurt in the process does not matter. Makes no sense, right? Who would hurt their own kids just to screw with their ex-spouse? A narcissist will absolutely do it, so be ready for it.

My deep love for my children was a target for Gigi. Making my kids confused and angry was a tool she used to get to me, and for a long time it was effective. I remember my daughter Elisha coming to me one evening. She had been acting very standoffish since returning from a visit with her mother,

"Dad, why do you smoke pot every day? Doing drugs is against the law, and I hate people who smoke weed."

She was a teenager at the time, so she definitely had her voice. "Mom told me about all your girlfriends. No wonder she didn't trust you."

I was totally pissed off and called Gigi to give her a piece of my mind. "Why would you tell the kids I smoke weed every day? That is such bullshit, and you know how they feel about drugs! Telling them about my ex-girlfriends and my past is fucking insane! What the hell are you thinking?!"

Chalk that speech up to a narcissist, one and you, zero! You won't win—and neither will your kids. All you can do is talk to your kids and let them know the truth, and hopefully they will get it. Don't try to fight fire with fire; it only hurts your children.

Here is an important lesson I learned. If you give a narcissist the satisfaction of showing how angry you are by teeing off on them, you are the loser! Don't do it. Don't yell, don't scream, just drop it.

The one thing that you can and must expect: Your kids will be used as pawns. You are in a game you cannot win.

Some examples of what to expect:

If your spouse is supposed to take the children for the weekend, and the kids are excited about it, planned for it . . . well, expect that it won't happen.

What You Need to Know: Am I Dealing with a Narcissist?

If they are supposed to pick up the kids at 9 AM, and they know you have something to do, expect them to be there at noon.

If they are supposed to have the kids back to you by 8:30 PM on a school night, expect them at midnight. Maybe later.

When I would tell friends or family about the things Gigi was doing, the reaction was always the same. "What the hell is wrong with her? Is she on drugs? Goddamn Shane, didn't you see this shit when you were married to her?"

Their reactions were always the same and, to be honest, my wife freaked me out. I was afraid of her. Gigi didn't seem to care that what she was doing was hurting our children. When she was flying with her boyfriend, she'd go days without calling or talking to the kids. It was a complete 180-degree change, and the kids didn't know what to make of it; and I couldn't explain it to them. When she did see our children, she was often very short with them, and things would end with her becoming angry, walking away and leaving them in tears. It was a constant struggle to keep the kids upright.

The Fact I Needed to Realize

It didn't matter that we'd spent many great years together bringing up three beautiful kids, traveling the world, enjoying first birthday parties, kindergarten graduations, gymnastics, and martial arts from white belt to black belt. The very happy times and the very sad times that made up the family we once were . . . no longer mattered. With all of that between us, how in God's name could she turn on me?

I can't emphasize this enough, so please try to internalize what I am about to tell you. Narcissism is a serious personality disorder for which there is no cure. Well, actually, that's not accurate. *Theoretically*, if a narcissist understands that they have this personality disorder, and dedicate themselves to fixing the problem, they can be cured. The problem is that ego will never allow them to admit to the disorder.

At that time I didn't understand NPD. As I look back now, after reading books and talking to professionals dealing with the disorder on a firsthand basis, I know that Gigi is a narcissist. Dr. Faith was always reluctant to make a diagnosis of Gigi, but there were countless times when I would tell her how Gigi was acting, and she would say, "That is classic narcissism."

The narcissist is the most important person on the planet, and they are above everyone else.

Especially you.

Many good books and articles are available about NPD and dealing with a narcissist. A good video series that proved to be invaluable to me was by a life coach named Stephanie Lyn. Just search her name online, and you'll find a lot of helpful videos on the subject.

If you are, in fact, dealing with a narcissist, the sooner you understand and accept this, the sooner you'll be able to move forward. I was dealing with a personality disorder, but I couldn't bring myself to fully embrace this fact until well after the final divorce decree had been issued. If I'd been able to fully grasp this early on, I know my divorce would have been more manageable for me, and it also may have been less stressful on my kids.

There's only one thing that I know of that puts you slightly ahead of the game when dealing with NPD. The single thing you can and should do is to *move on*.

The sooner you can get emotionally past your ex, the better. As soon as you can go on with your life—or at least to appear to have done so—you'll see a decline in the attacks. Nothing else will make it happen. You must make it apparent that what they are doing is not getting to you, is not affecting you. Once that happens you'll see the attacks slow down. It might never stop but it does slow down.

As I write this book, it's been over five years since Gigi walked out the door; and to this day, she expresses nothing but hate toward me.

What You Need to Know: Am I Dealing with a Narcissist?

On the occasion that I see her at one of my kid's sporting events, award ceremony, or graduation, the look on her face says it all: *I hate you, Shane.* In Gigi's eyes, I *have* to be the bad guy. If it weren't my fault, then it would have to be her fault—and that is impossible. So regardless of how good a husband and father I had been, to her, I am now evil.

Early on Gigi would text and email me hate speech. She would say abusive things like, "You are a fucking loser and will never amount to anything! I am so glad I will never have to look at your ugly face ever again!"

It wasn't until I stopped feeding her need for negative energy that she completely stopped talking to me. This happened after the divorce was finalized. Her not speaking to me has its advantages, but I wanted to co-parent with her, and the lack of communication made this impossible. Everything I'd read in all the literature about children of divorce screams to communicate with your ex for the sake of the children. But, to this day there is no substantive communication between us.

When all is said and done and the final bell is sounded—regardless of the results—you are and will remain despised.

For a narcissist, the idea that "time heals all wounds" is not a thing.

Communication

Can you completely cut off all communications? No, but when you do communicate, keep it to the bare minimum; and no matter how confrontational they are, no matter how shitty they have treated you or your kids, your response should be short and to the point.

Never embellish or add narrative to a question. *Yes* and *no* are great words to remember and use when texting a response. Keep it as brief and to the point as possible.

SHANE O'BRIAN

My Mental Health

I remember telling friends how I felt. "It's like being on the octopus ride at Six Flags, and I can't get off."

The Octopus is one of those rides you can climb on at any county fair or amusement park. Can you imagine it? Eight arms spinning around with four seats twirling at the end of each arm. It gets you dizzy as heck and makes you feel nauseated—or actually makes you puke. That's exactly how I felt. Never ending spinning.

Even though everyone, including Dr. Faith told me, "Shane do not engage her—do not let her know she is getting to you . . ."

I'd say, "It's my kids' lives here—I need to fight for them."

My hope is that if you're dealing with a narcissist, you'll be able to recognize that by now, and ultimately save yourself a ton of heartache and pain. You're not going crazy; you are not a bad person. You are not alone. The opposite is true! So breathe, don't react.

Hope for the best; expect the worst.

Chapter Three
Takeaways and Action Items

- Keep communications clean and simple. You do not need to embellish your responses or revist old arguments. A simple yes or no can be great responses.

- Emotions can be very strong, and strong emotions are easily pulled into arguments.

- Remember your exercises and other training to help you stay calm and not engage.

- Not every ex is a narcissist, but it's helpful to recognize the signs of Narcissistic Personality Disorder (NPD). Common signs include: inflated self image, inability to negotiate, lack of empathy; use of children as a weapon.

- Understand and minimize narcissistic supply—both positive and negative.

- Move on, or, at a minimum, make it appear that you have moved on.

- If your spouse's behavior is getting to you, concentrate on the practices you've put in place and any good things you're doing for yourself. If they make you crazy, you'll make poor decisions, so work to stay healthy and sane.

CHAPTER FOUR

FINDING A LAWYER

As we weave our way through this thing called life, we inevitably will need the counsel of a professional. Choose wisely.

There's no shortage of divorce lawyers in the small community where I live. Some are notorious for being cutthroat, while others have a decent reputation as good negotiators. Some are known for being good at representing women, and others are known for representing men. Ask around and I'm sure you'll hear the good, the bad, and the ugly of the divorce attorneys in your area. Generally speaking, divorce lawyers have a well-deserved bad reputation.

One of the first things I found out—in my area, at least—is that if you go and speak with a lawyer about your case, that lawyer cannot represent your spouse. So, if there's a hard-hitting lawyer in your community who's famous for being cutthroat, go talk to that one first.

I again turned to my corporate attorney friend Sam for advice on who I should contact for representation. I let him know what was going on and how instantly things had become extremely contentious. Sam had known Gigi and me for years and was aware of my family situation. He also knew my kids.

He said, "Shane, I handle a lot of divorces, but I don't do contested divorces; and yours sounds like it may turn into a battle."

He gave me the names of a few people, but he said hands down, the most ruthless attorney on the block is Kory Kline. Everyone knows of him simply as K. I made the appointment that day and went to see him.

Interviewing a few top lawyers is a must, if, for no other reason than you take them off the list of lawyers your spouse can choose for representation.

An attorney will have some questions for you, and as long as there's no conflict of interest in representing you, they'll simply tell you what their retainer is. Once you pay that—**bam**—you have yourself a lawyer.

Opting for the hard-hitting attorney has its advantages, but if you are divorcing a narcissist, an ultra-aggressive lawyer can be counterproductive. A more reasonable negotiator might be the better choice. A narcissist thrives on conflict and feels that the more expensive it is for you, the better. A ruthless lawyer is going to keep the argument going and enjoy fighting the never-ending fight. Since I wasn't fully aware of Gigi's mental state, when I was seeking representation, I didn't take this into consideration.

I did interviews with a few lawyers, but in the end, I chose K. I'd known him a bit in social circles, and he was considered to be the number-one divorce attorney in my area.

Financing Your Divorce

Lawyers are expensive, and your finances at the beginning of a divorce can be a complete nightmare. Preparing for the move to Oregon and putting the down payment on the house in Portland had tied up most of my available cash. When I realized I just couldn't handle everything on my own and I needed some relief from the financial stress, I had to borrow $10,000 from a friend. I hope you have some resources you can tap into to get the ball rolling. Often, it's family that comes to the financial rescue. This is another layer of stress on your shoulders, but know that you're going to get through this.

It was the day after Gigi cancelled the mediation—for the fourth time—that I found myself in K's office. We talked about the fees and charges I'd be paying and what I could expect from them and what they expected of me. I gave him the retainer of $5,000. This was to be the first of far too many payments I'd be making to K's office.

Preparing to File for Divorce

Preparing for filing the "Complaint for Divorce, Child Custody, and Support" papers took all the energy and concentration I could muster. This is the time that you will need access to all your financial files. If you've been good with record keeping throughout your marriage, you're miles ahead of the game. I'd worked for myself for a very long time—owned my own company—so I had been using accounting software for many years. I had good records, but it was still a lot of work putting everything together and compiling all the information for my lawyer.

You will need to compile the following information for your first meeting with your attorney:

- Several months of all bank statements, including personal, corporate, and joint accounts. Be sure to have a couple of months prior to separation and up to the current date.
- All credit card statements for personal and joint credit cards. Again, include a couple of months of statements prior to separation and up to the current date. If you have access to your partner's statements you should include them.

- All loan information: personal, corporate, mortgage, and car loans. Be aware of who has been paying what and for how long and what accounts were being used to make those payments.
- Note all automobile information to include any remaining balance on any loan, the current blue book value of the auto, and who is using the car.
- Your home is your biggest asset. If you own a home, copy three months of the most recent statements and include them in the packet for the attorney. You may ask a real estate agent for an estimate of the current market value of your home. A ballpark figure is all you need.
- Any other asset you may have, a second home, rental income, boats, trucks, and expensive toys like personal watercraft or ATVs should all be listed. Your soon to be ex-wife's shoe collection is not considered an asset.
- Include your most recent two to three months of check stubs. If you work for yourself, include all information on your income. In my case, that meant copies of a few months of my gross receipt taxes. The way you track your income and that of your company may vary from place to place. Just ask your attorney what's needed.
- I was asked to bring in my previous three years of tax returns. If you've filed jointly with your spouse, take those. If you filed separately and you have access to your spouse's records, take both returns. If you own your own company, the corporate taxes will be necessary as well.
- Gather all the information on any costs related to your children. School tuition, extracurricular activity cost, and any special care or expense that can be attributed to the care of your children counts. For example, if your child needs special care or a regiment of drugs due to a long-term illness, this should be documented.

Finding a Lawyer

- Make a basic inventory of household items of value that are jointly owned. Include an estimate of the purchase price and current worth.
- Be sure to note which one of you is responsible for any recurring bills.
- Make copies of everything and put it together in a comprehensive package with a summary page so it's easy for your attorney to understand. Your lawyer will charge you by the minute, so having your records in order and easy to understand will help minimize the fee they will be hitting you with.

I gathered all the info while also dealing with the daily drama of crying children. Under any other circumstance, all the financial record gathering and putting together a comprehensive picture of my finances would have been easy, but at this time it was overwhelming.

After assembling the package, I met with K again and went over the entire picture. We also discussed everything that had transpired in my marriage, our plans to move to Portland, the day Gigi told me about her affair . . . it was so difficult to spell all this out to people I didn't really know, but it was a fact of my life by then.

K prepared and filed the "Complaint for Divorce, Child Custody, and Support" roughly seven weeks after Gigi dropped the "I want a divorce" bomb on all of us. It took another two weeks after that for her attorney to submit the "Answer to Complaint for Divorce and Counterclaim." This was the first real hint of what was to come. Their counterclaim was filled with lies such as denial of any adultery, which laid the groundwork for her to begin the claim that she was forced out of the house by me, a habitual drug addict with a complete inability to parent a hamster, let alone three children. It wasn't December 7, 1941, but it sure felt like the start of the war.

Life at Home

While all the legal battles were starting, circumstances around my home were getting worse. My kids were not doing well, and to have one of them crying all night was not out of the norm. Gigi had moved in with her boyfriend and refused to be civil in any way. She also refused to let me know when she wanted to see the kids. To her, it was none of my business and she didn't need to clear anything with me.

My kids were developing some serious health and emotional issues. They were aged fifteen, thirteen, and eight at the time. Imagine how hard it was on them. This went on for weeks, and when things seemingly started to normalize, my ex decided that when her boyfriend was out of town, she would be moving back into our house. I couldn't allow that to happen. I begged her family members, all of whom I had known for decades, to intervene. I asked that they stop her from trying to move back in. They all agreed that it would be harmful to the children. I thought I could count on my in-laws for some sanity, but there was something else I found out the hard way: most people do not want to get involved. They see it as a no-win for themselves, so they simply look the other way. I warned Gigi's mom, brother, and sister that I would file a restraining order, but they either didn't believe me or felt their hands were tied.

If you are close with your in-laws, keep in mind that, regardless of the relationship you've shared with them over the years, blood is thicker than water.

I told Gigi there was no way I would allow her to move back in. "Are you kidding? The kids are just getting used to things. They cry every night, and now you think you can come and go in and out of this house all while you're living with your boyfriend? Seriously? Hell no, Gigi, there's no way you're going to do that to the kids or to me—so figure out something else."

"Listen, you fucking jerk, that is as much my house as it is yours, so get over it. I'll be staying in the office. if you don't like it, get the fuck out!"

"Gigi, this is going to turn out really bad, so don't even try it."

"Kiss my ass, Shane."

Gigi was never shy about how she expressed herself, but her language and attitude had become radically different. I wasn't dealing with my wife any longer. I felt as though I was dealing with a foulmouthed, angry drug dealer in New York City. I didn't know how to react.

Shortly after my argument with Gigi, I remember having a conversation with her mother. I begged her to talk to her daughter about the issue. She said something to me that stopped me in my tracks, something that forever made me look at that woman in a completely different light.

"Mom, Gigi is sleeping with a married man, which is adultery and a mortal sin in your religion. Do you really expect me to allow her to come live here while she is sleeping with another man? That is out of the question."

"Shane, this is her house too, and she can come and go as she pleases; and besides, there is always a reason for adultery."

It was at that moment I realized what I had to do. It was a heart wrenching decision, but I called my lawyer and made the appointment to see him first thing in the morning.

We met right after I dropped the kids at school. I was so torn up by the drama and turmoil that I really thought I was starting to lose my mind. I told K what was going on, and told him I wanted to file a restraining order to keep Gigi away from the kids and the house. We talked about the several instances when Gigi had slapped Elisha and how I'd had to get between them. K told me he would file the necessary paperwork. Once a judge agreed to allow it, Gigi would be served the papers.

K asked me where Gigi could be located, and I gave him the address of her mom's house, sister's house, and boyfriend's house. The marshall caught up to her at her mother's house. I guess having her served in front of "There is always a reason for adultery" was a bit of poetic justice.

Although Gigi had been having an affair and had essentially turned her back on my children and me, this was my kid's mother. I was taking away my children's ability to see their mom, and I didn't take this fact lightly. As I look back at it, I know that I did what I had to do. I also know that Gigi used it as a weapon against me with my kids. She made my daughter feel responsible for her being unable to return to her home. The restraining order was predicated on the issue that Gigi had been slapping Elisha. I know that Elisha still feels she's at fault.

Advice about You and Your Attorney

This is something that took me a long time to realize; and I would like to emphasize this point here. Your attorney works for *you*. If your attorney is like ninety-five percent of others in the industry, he's a know-it-all asshole. They are often self-absorbed jerks who can be very narcissistic. Imagine that. While they *are* the experts, and they have likely gone through countless divorces, it doesn't mean they can drive this bus the way they want to without you having a say in it. Educate yourself, and when you feel strongly about something—make them listen to you and don't back down. You're paying them $250 per hour (or whatever outrageous fee your lawyer charges), and they better listen and do what you instruct them to do.

Be mindful that the lawyers in your community all deal with one another over and over in court—and oftentimes they're friends. If your lawyer or the opposing counsel drops the ball by not turning in required information to the court, it will cause delays. The resulting reworking of documents and updating of financial information can get very expensive. It can become a nightmare. And because the judges and lawyers are all in the system together, no one wants to make the other look bad in court. After all, when O'Brian v. O'Brian is done, they have to continue to work with—or against—that other lawyer. So when you see that things have been mishandled either by your attorney, the opposing attorney, or the judge, document it. *Demand* that your attorney listen to you and abide by your wishes. Make note of any deadlines set by the judge and make sure your attorney files everything with the court in a timely manner. Before you waste your time going to see the judge, make sure the opposing counsel has filed what they are supposed to file.

It doesn't matter that you've submitted everything on time, and you've done your part to move the process forward. If either attorney fails to submit to the court the financial worksheet or turn in their rebuttal in time for the judge to properly review it, the process will be delayed again and again. This can all add up to . . . your kids' college fund getting screwed out of another $2,000 by two assholes who are friends and are making a killing by kicking the can down the road at your expense. Stand up and tell them, "Hell no!"

During my divorce, one of my many mistakes or lapses in judgment was that I didn't watch the billing from my attorney close enough. Just looking at the bill, watching my children's savings get wasted away, added to my already super stressful life, so I was irresponsible. Don't be like me. Watch the bills coming in from your attorney; and if you think something is amiss, make a note of it.

I will not have you without the darkness that hides within you.
I will not let you have me without the madness that makes me.
If our demons cannot dance, neither can we. —Nikita Gill

Chapter Four
Takeaways and Action Items

- Ask around about attorneys in your area and interview some of the top lawyers.

- After retaining a lawyer, prepare information needed for your first meeting.

- Find the previous three years of tax returns, either jointly filed or individual returns.

- Prepare your year-to-date income information. Your previous three months of check stubs or similar records should do it.

- Create a list of all your assets: home(s), vehicles, rental properties, retirement accounts, luxury items, or anything that may be deemed an asset. Get a ballpark idea of what each asset is worth.

- Create a list of all your liabilities: credit cards, auto loans, home loans, personal or corporate loans, and so on. Several months of statements would be helpful. Make a note of who pays for loans and credit cards, how they are paid, and through which bank accounts they are paid.

- Create a list of all your bank accounts: personal accounts, joint accounts, corporate accounts, and anything else. Note who pays into the accounts and what each account is used for in paying the bills.

- List all child-related expenses. Be sure to include school tuition, daycare, extracurricular activities, medical needs, incidentals, gifts, and so on. Make notes about who pays for it and which accounts are used.

- Start an events journal so you have a place to write things down as they happen. If you can make notes as events happen, great. If not, it's a good idea to take a few minutes at the end of the day to go over what happened. Note when your attorney or opposing counsel does—or does not—take care of necessary filings. Note when your spouse fails to do what they are supposed to with the children's care. Note what your children are saying and how they're acting.

- Gather all your material in a three-ring binder or folder. Everything should be in order and easy to understand with a summary cover sheet.

CHAPTER FIVE

BARGAINING: TRYING TO END THE INSANITY

"Babe, please think this through. We're a family. You can't turn away from that. I still love you, and I can forgive you. We need to work this out for the sake of the kids. You can't just leave us."

After denial, when you couldn't accept this was happening to you and knew you didn't deserve it, you moved on to anger. You were mad at your ex, mad at the circumstance you and your children were thrown into, and at times even mad at God for letting this happen to your family. And then comes the next stage.

Bargaining (Stage 3)

In bargaining, the third stage in grieving the breakup of your marriage and family, you try to make deals to make everything go back to normal. The acts of going to a marriage counselor and mediation are all part of the bargaining stage.

Looking back at how things unfolded, the emotions I felt never really took on a specific singular emotion at any given time. Denial was one emotion that did dissipate quickly because the roller coaster I was on was so *undeniably* terrible. To deny the obvious was not an option for very long. Anger is an emotion that, at times, I still feel to this day. It's not that I dwell on being angry, or that I yell and scream and stomp my feet in fits of rage; but there are still times when my ex does something needlessly vindictive, hurting my children, that my emotions well up.

How you handle your emotions as they come to you and how you move through them may depend on how introspective you are. You must be willing to look inside yourself and let the feelings take their course. How quickly or slowly the emotions rear their ugly heads is not something anyone can predict. You may have relapses into denial and anger throughout your journey—this is okay and it's normal. Don't be too hard on yourself.

I think I stayed in the bargaining stage the longest. Divorce was a painful experience, and I was driven to do things that I wish I hadn't had to do. But even during those times of being furious with the situation, I longed to have my family back. I wanted the entire situation to stop—and to that end I bargained with my ex up until the trial started.

Initially, I did want to keep Gigi in my life. I had always thought that if I ever found out she was fooling around (she is a flight attendant after all, I am not completely naïve), I'd be able to drop her like a hot rock. Well, it wasn't like that. For a very long time I considered her my best friend; walking away from that was hard. The first month or so after she left, I truly wanted her back. With that said, it honestly didn't take very long until I saw how truly evil she was; so wanting her back dissipated relatively quickly, especially when you consider we'd been married for over twenty years.

I continued to bargain because I wanted to be able to sit down with Gigi and have dinner with her and the kids in a family-type atmosphere. I could take the loss of my wife, but I didn't want to accept

Bargaining: Trying to End the Insanity

the loss of my family. I remember writing settlement proposals that would take the situation out of the court and (hopefully) stop the lawyers from pitting us against each other. Gigi and I had become enemies; and while I now understand why, at the time I wanted to make things better for my grieving children. On some level I thought that Gigi and I could be friends, or at least be civil for the kids' sake.

I spent a lot of time and a lot of money drafting proposals. At first, K was involved, and he advised me. We never got a decent response from any of Gigi's lawyers, and K was much quicker than I was to realize what a waste of time and effort it was. He tried to warn me, but I was stubborn and hoped to take things out of the lawyers' and court's hands. It never worked.

As I look back at the resolutions, I know that it was really an act of desperation. I desperately wanted the divorce to go away. I wanted to stop the crazy waste of money, and I never wanted to go back to court again.

I have to admit to myself that my many attempts to bargain with Gigi were the wrong thing to do because it kept me engaged with a person who would never compromise and would use my attempts at a sane solution against me. It was the narcissism in Gigi that I was fighting. There's no win when you're fighting that.

This is not to say that *you* can't bargain with *your* spouse. Give it your best effort and leave the anger and hate behind when you're seeking a compromise. Know that money has very little importance in the big scheme of things. Do your best.

You expect the world to have your values
To look on the brighter side and take joy in every day
To understand that the gift of now is a blessing
And the promise of tomorrow, you can only pray.

Chapter Five

Takeaways and Action Items

- The emotional rollercoaster doesn't stop when the first flush of anger and denial start to fade. Remember that you might—and probably will—have those feelings come back.

- You might be the best deal-maker in the world, but you can't bargain past a spouse who has made up their mind to leave.

- Also, you can't bargain with God to make things go back to how they were.

- Remember that you need to take care of yourself and your children. Any bargain you make needs to honor these priorities.

CHAPTER SIX

TELLING THE KIDS

As I looked into the eyes of my innocent children,
I knew that their innocence had been stolen.
It's a moment in time I can never forget,
And till death and beyond, I shall always regret.

Before I get into the worst day of my life, I'll let you know how I prepared for it. A good friend of mine went through a terrible divorce (everyone has a few friends like that); and he told me that in his area when you file for divorce, all parents must complete a class in how to care for the children of divorce. Your jurisdiction may or may not mandate this, but many areas in the U.S. require it. The name of the program is *Children in Between*. Although it's not required where I live, I went ahead and paid for the program and went on to take the class.

The course is comprehensive and provides all the dos and don'ts. It includes videos of people handling conversations with their children regarding the other parent. Dropping off the kids, picking them up, using the kids as messengers . . . It shows how terrible we can all be without knowing it. After I paid for the course, I gave Gigi the web address, log-in name, and password, then asked that she please look it over.

"I don't need your bullshit, Shane! The kids are fine!"

We were still in the beginning stages of the upheaval of our family. It was maybe two or three weeks into the process that I knew the kids needed to be told the truth. They saw things get bad extremely quickly. Adding to the fact that their mother and I were separating and their mom had a new boyfriend, I also had to tell them that we were no longer moving to Portland. Talk about getting the rug pulled out from under you. This was the trifecta of fucked up. Leading up to the time I knew I'd gather them all together to share the heartbreaking news was agony.

There's nothing I can say that will prepare you for the task of telling your children about the separation or divorce. Seriously, writing about this years later still brings a tear to my eye.

My three beautiful and innocent children sat with me in the living room. While I tried to remain strong, I had already been crying; and I knew that I looked like a wreck. It was all I could do to speak.

"Hey guys, I have some stuff to tell you. This is adult stuff, and I wish to God I didn't have to say all this, but I want you to know what is going on; and I want you to know that I will do everything I can to make this better. You know your mom and I have been having problems. Your mom isn't happy being married to me. She loves you all and will always be your mother, but she doesn't want to be with me anymore."

The look on my children's faces was as though they had just been slapped. My daughter looked defiant and angry. My sons were both in shock. They saw the tears rolling down my face, and I don't know if they started crying because I was sobbing, or if it was the brick that had just fallen on top of their heads that hurt.

I had talked to Dr. Faith and everyone I knew who had gone through anything close to my situation, and the consensus was to tell the kids that their mom was with someone else. They were going to find out eventually; and as this was the main reason for the separation and impending divorce, I thought that the truth was the best route to take. To this day I'm not sure if that moment was the right time . . . but then again, when would the right time ever have come?

"Your mom loves someone else and will be living with him while we figure out what to do next. We are talking to some really smart people, and they are helping us. We won't be moving to Portland, and you'll all be going back to your own schools, and we'll be staying in this house for now."

There was a lot of crying, some yelling from my daughter, and a lot of hugs. The anguish they felt kept us all up until the wee hours of the morning. Looking back, I'd equate this situation to telling loved ones that their parents had died. I'd later realize that the finality of death of a loved one is a much easier pill to swallow than the death of your family.

Elisha, berated me, "You can fix this, Dad! Make it right!"

I guess this is what Don Henley meant when he wrote, *The End of the Innocence*. If you don't know the song or forgot the lyrics, take time to have a listen to it. It's such a beautifully sad song—and it fits.

This will not make any of this easier, but the fact is, more than half the kids graduating from high school in the U.S. have gone through divorce at some point in their lives. It's not always as bad as what my family endured, but this is a story that could be told over and over. Do your best to work with your ex to make it as easy on the kids as possible.

Basic rules of behavior when dealing with your children who are going through divorce:

Rule #1: Make sure the kids know it's not their fault. Kids will believe that if they had behaved better, or earned better grades, or didn't cause Mom and Dad argue so much about them, things would be different. No matter the actual circumstances, kids think they're to blame.

Let them know that you and your spouse are the adults, you love them, and it's absolutely not their fault.

Rule #2: Don't talk shit about your ex or their paramour.

Rule #3: Don't put the kids in the middle or expect them to be messengers for you. If you have something to communicate with your ex, then you—and you alone—should communicate it, preferably not within hearing distance of the children.

Here are some examples of what not to say:

"Tell your mother to pay the goddamn car payment! I told her it was her responsibility, and now my credit is fucked because of her!"

"Tell your screwed-up father that he and his bitch better be on time to pick you up this week—or he's not taking you at all!"

Something that I had to learn on the fly was how to handle everything concerning the kids by myself. When issues arose with them, I no longer had a spouse to bounce things off. And, of course, at this very difficult time in their lives, a lot of problems needed to be dealt with.

I tried to communicate what was going on with the kids and how hurt they were. There were signs, both physical and emotional, that my children were under more stress than they could handle, and I was on my own to figure out how best to help them cope.

Gigi was suddenly living a high-flying lifestyle with the new freedom of not having to hide her affair. Instead of making time for the kids, she was taking trips with her lover every chance she had. Instead of helping her kids adjust to their new reality, getting them ready for school, supporting her teenage daughter with the girl issues that came up just wasn't something she thought was important. I knew the kids felt abanconed, and it made it that much harder to accept this life changing event. An event they neither asked for nor wanted.

I painstakingly communicated to Gigi everything that was going on with the kids. I emailed her about the boys crying because she hadn't called in days and I didn't know how to explain it to them. I told her how Elisha was acting out and hollering at me for one reason or another. Looking back, I know that keeping Gigi abreast of what was happening with the kids was counterproductive. I learned (in one of the many books I read) that if you want to make someone mad, tell them a lie, if you want to make a narcissist mad, tell them the truth. Gigi didn't want to hear the truth.

My basic point here is that you and your spouse are adults—so act like it. Help each other with the children. Be there for your kids. During this time, work doesn't matter. Your golf game doesn't matter, and neither does your hair appointment. What matters is the sanity of your offspring.

Counseling for the Children

During this season, there were a couple things I did that I'm still not sure about—whether they helped or made things worse. Everyone I spoke to and everything I read screamed to me that children going through divorce must see a professional to help them work through the tragedy.

The kids were all against it. But I begged and bribed them to indulge me and talk to a therapist. I explained that I was worried and wanted them to have someone to open up to. I pointed out that I was seeing Dr. Faith and how much it had already helped me. My daughter was scared to go because she thought if any of her classmates found out that she was seeing a psychologist, she would be ostracized. My boys didn't like the thought of it either. Daniel had just turned thirteen and John was only eight when their mom left. I can't imagine what they thought when I told them I wanted them to talk to a psychologist. Gigi was totally against the idea, which made it all that much harder. I persevered and all three kids started seeing a child psychologist who Dr. Faith had recommended. I went in and met with Dr. Janet Spencer a week before the kids were to start. She was a very nice lady and I took the time to explain all that was happening and the issues the kids were facing. Dr. Janet was about my age and had worked in the field for decades so I was confident. She wanted to meet with Gigi so I gave her all the contact information and followed up with her in an email and copied Gigi on it. The kids were to see the therapist once a week.

After the kids had finished a session with Dr. Janet, I'd speak with her. I got some invaluable insight from this very kind woman. It was important to share with the psychologist the issues I was having with our new family dynamic and how the kids were letting out their anger and frustration. Also, I made sure the kids didn't think that everything that they told to the therapist was being relayed back to their mother and me. I never told the kids what the therapist said to me and would never allude to something in my conversations with my kids about what Dr. Janet had told me.

One way the psychologist tried to get the kids to open up was through art. She'd ask them to draw pictures of how they felt. After one particular session, Dr. Janet showed me a picture my precious John had drawn. It was as sad a drawing as I'd ever seen. A little boy standing at the edge of a dark field—no trees or birds, just a cloud-filled day in near dark with a small child all alone, head down. The caption read, "I miss my family." I remember that the three kids were sitting in the clinic waiting room while I spoke to the psychologist, and it took me twenty minutes to pull myself together enough to walk out of the office. It was one of many times that the sheer sorrow my children were going through had a profound effect on me.

It's important you're aware that a therapist may be called to testify or offer written testimony to the court about the psychological well-being of your child.

During the course of my divorce proceedings, the kids' therapist was called upon and offered two written testimonies at the behest of the court. Each time, Dr. Janet was careful not to take sides in the divorce. In her written testimony she noted that the kids were having a hard time with the family structure change and that therapy should continue. She also mentioned that my daughter did not want to meet her mother's boyfriend. I am sure that fact was a point of contention between Gigi and Elisha.

Aside from the trips to the psychologist, one other thing I did may have been an overreach now that I look back. I started taking the kids to church. While they had gone before and this was not new, it was new to go with Dad. Their mom being the good Christian woman that she is, would take them to church from time to time—or when my mother-in-law demanded it. It was probably not the best idea, but I was desperate for the kids to start healing and to help them find hope and love and maybe God. The kids didn't take to it, so after a year of Sunday morning mass, I relented. The kids never asked why we stopped going to church. I think they were just happy to sleep in on Sunday morning. I had changed the kids' normal routine, and maybe that just wasn't the right thing to do.

Talking to the Teachers

Gigi asked for a divorce at the beginning of summer. When it came time to get my children back into school, I had to tell the teachers and principal what was going on. My daughter was re-enrolled in an all-girls Catholic school. I went and met with the principal and I explained that my girl may be absentminded or act out a bit. I asked her to call me if anything came up. My boys were entering fourth and eighth grades at the Christian school they'd attended since kindergarten. I met with the pastor and with each of their teachers to share what was happening. I felt it was very important and asked all concerned to contact me if they noticed any problems.

It was difficult for me to talk with the teachers and let them know about our present circumstance. Again, I had to pause often to gather myself as I told these strangers how devastated my children were. None of the kids did well in school that year, and I kept the expectations low. I gave praise for the B's and C's on each of their report cards, knowing full well that the previous year the lowest grade any of them had earned was a B+. The signs that the divorce was taking a severe toll on the kids were obvious.

My word of advice on dealing with your children is this: Remember, they're only kids. Remember that, no matter what, they'll love your ex and they'll need both parents' acceptance. I've consistently stuck to the high ground when talking about and dealing with Gigi. I hope that, when my kids are grown and they look back, they'll be able to see I did my best.

The statistics about children that come from broken families aren't good. The fact that your children have gone through this horrible experience greatly increases their chances of having trouble in many facets of life. The list is long and depressing, but you should make yourself aware of the myriad of problems they face. Pray.

Your children will see how you and your spouse respond to each other during this conflict. Be aware that how you act toward the other parent *does* matter. A friend and a bit of a spiritual advisor of mine once told me, "Shane, be kind to those that don't deserve it."

At those times when things were bad and my kids were so hurt that I stayed up until 3 AM trying to get one of them to calm down, it was difficult to follow his suggestion. I admit there were times that I stumbled and let loose on my ex, but I never did it in front of the kids; and for the most part I was kind and still am. I can't say it has in any way made this journey better, but I can look at myself in the mirror and still like the person I see.

Telling the Kids

You have every right to be angry. Your children are crushed and your life is forever changed. Don't fight the feeling. Let it out. Tell your inner circle of friends and family how you are affected and get it out of your system.

One thing is certain, your children are going to be hurt in the process of divorce, and you can only try to ease their pain—and hopefully limit the uncertainty they must be feeling. This must coincide with your own acceptance of your circumstance.

Be kind to those that don't deserve it.

Chapter Six

Takeaways and Action Items

- Ask your attorney about any requirements in your area about parents with children going through divorce.

- Comply with any state or legal requirements regarding children and custody.

- Remember to write about your children in your journal.

- When telling the kids about a separation or divorce the basic rules are:

  o Let the children know it is not their fault.

  o Avoid speaking poorly about your spouse or their paramour.

  o Communicate as directly as you can with your spouse, and do not use the children as messengers when dealing with your spouse.

  o Get the children help in therapy. They may have a hard time dealing with their emotions, so try to be patient with them.

  o Remember, they are just children

  o Talk to teachers, coaches, and counselors who are dealing with your children. Let them know what is going on and that they can always contact you should there be any problems.

CHAPTER SEVEN

SEPARATING SPACE

Get the fuck out! Take your shit and get out of this house now!
I do not want to spend one more minute looking at your ugly face.
(This is an example of what not to say.)

However you put it, the act of separating is an immense undertaking and can be a heart-wrenching event in your—and more importantly, your children's—lives. As we go through our existence, there will inevitably be separation, and it is never easy.

It's around the time you file for divorce that you'll likely need to move out or have your spouse pack their things and vacate. It's also a time to separate all financial entanglements from your spouse. This stressful time can lead to contentious exchanges. You may be inclined to say or do some things that are out of character.

Separating will take every ounce of patience and understanding you can muster. The process needs to be handled delicately for you and your partner to move forward in a civil manner.

Moving Out

The act of physically moving out of a home that you love will test you. Be prepared for your emotions to spill over. If it's you who is vacating the home, remove all your belongings as quickly and with as little fanfare as possible. Hopefully, you and your spouse will both be reasonable. Likely, many jointly owned items will need to be considered. Furnishings, artwork, and appliances are all generally owned jointly. For the time being, just take what you need out of the house. Make notes and take photos of items you want as part of the divorce settlement. Photos will also help show the condition of the items at the time you leave the home. Put a date stamp on your photos. Dividing the property will be done through negotiation or, if need be, by the court.

If it's your spouse who is vacating, schedule a time that you'll be out of the house, and give them the time to collect their belongings and say goodbye to the home. Make absolutely no move to damage or destroy any of their belongings. The practical reason is that it will cost your ex money to replace these things, which, in the end, may cause hardship on your children.

You may feel compelled to keep or hide items that you bought for your spouse over the years. Although you may have paid for the watch, jewelry, or designer bag, those things should remain in possession of the person to whom they were given.

My Experience

A normal situation would have entailed my ex setting up a time to come to the house and pick up her belongings and take them out. My divorce was a lot of things; normal was not one of them.

I'm jumping forward a bit, as the separating of space and getting my ex to actually remove her belongings from the family home took well over a year. Here is how it eventually climaxed.

Separating Space

I have a nice place in a gated community. The fact that Gigi didn't want to see me in the home for one more day was very apparent by both her words and actions.

"That is my fucking house, and you are going to live there over my dead body! Put it on the market and sell it!"

Besides all the beautiful sculptures and paintings that we'd collected over many years of travel, there was also Gigi's massive shoe collection, dress collection, tons of designer jeans, brand-name bags, scarves, and more workout outfits than Jane Fonda could go through in a lifetime . . . You get the picture. It was a lot of stuff.

When Gigi left to go live with her boyfriend, she took only a fraction of her possessions. I asked her to get her belongings out, but she refused. Early in the court proceedings the judge told her to take her things out of the house and gave her a timeline to follow. The judge spelled it all out. I told Gigi that she could take any of the artwork or furnishings she wanted. She absolutely refused to remove anything from the house.

Throughout the ordeal she was either receiving some really crappy advice, or she was just stubborn. It was probably a lot of both.

I think she felt that if she kept her things in the house . . . the house remained hers. We were joint owners after all, so in her mind the judge didn't have the right to tell her anything. She refused to follow the judge's orders.

Fast-forward fifteen months from our first hearing.

I was not trying to be unreasonable, but Gigi's clothes took up seventy-five percent of the master closet, and her shoe collection took up one hundred percent of the hallway closet space. I emailed Gigi and explained my plan to handle the situation. Due to some seasonal work I do, the storage unit I was renting would be empty during the Christmas holiday. I explained to Gigi that I would be packing her belongings into boxes and putting them into the storage—and she would have to remove them by New Years Eve, or I would donate everything to a charity. I also gave her other options: she could come by the house and pick up the things, or I was even willing to deliver the boxes to her residence. What do you suppose she did? Nope! Worse.

I got an email from K with a forwarded email from Gigi's lawyer (at this point she was on her third lawyer) which basically said that my threatening to dump all of his clients' belongings on the front yard of her residence was way out of line and would be brought up to the judge forthwith. K was not happy with me until I showed him the actual email I had written. K forwarded my email to the opposing counsel with a note that said, "If I were Shane, I would have put her shit in the garbage eight months ago! Tell your client to get her crap out of Shane's house; otherwise I don't care what he does with it!"

K had his moments.

After I packed up the sixteen, extra-large cardboard moving boxes with Gigi's overpriced and unused belongings, I took it to the storage locker. I gave Gigi the code to get through the gate, gave her the combination to the lock on the unit door, and went on about my business. She did get the stuff out by New Year's Eve. I later saw the attendant at the facility, and he told me about the rude and angry lady who went to my storage unit.

I apologized and said, "That's my ex."

He said, "You're lucky to be rid of that shit, dude."

I smiled and agreed.

Throughout the divorce, I always reminded Gigi that the house isn't mine as much as it is the kids' home. It's where they'd lived for the past ten years, a place they all loved. To demand that we move was insane.

Her response never changed, "That's my fucking house, and you will not be there in one year! I guarantee you that!"

Despite Gigi's predictions, the kids and I did stay in the house, which hopefully made this terrible part of their lives a little bit easier.

Financial Entanglements

During divorce, even if the negotiations with your spouse are going well, it's still a good idea to get your own bank accounts and credit cards that are solely in your name. If you trust your ex, then do it all as peacefully as you can. If you don't trust them, cancel joint credit cards and close bank accounts as soon as possible.

After twenty years of marriage, our finances were completely intertwined. Untangling them proved to be a monumental task. If you have doubts about what to do, consult with your attorney.

In a perfect world, splitting up assets and liabilities is easy and you'll both have funds to continue on with your separate lives. However, it's far more common for one spouse to try taking advantage of the situation. What once was a shared expense may now be solely your responsibility, which can make life even more stressful.

The most important thing about separating assets is keeping your records straight. If you take funds from a joint bank account, you must show what those funds were used for. If you close an account, keeping the bank statements in order will be necessary for the final separation of assets. If your ex goes on a shopping spree with your credit card, then—after first cancelling the card—print out the statement showing what the funds were used for. This type of thing happens all the time; but in the end, the lawyers or the court will iron it out as long as you have proof of a problem.

Keeping a Journal

I strongly recommend that you write things down as much as possible. Keep a journal and try to add to it every two or three days. Make note of anything important going on with the kids and everything that's going on with your finances as it relates to the divorce and your children. Write a summary of important conversations you have with your ex, your lawyer, the kids' therapist, and anything else that's important in your day-to-day life. If you get a nasty text or email from your ex (or worse, their paramour), be sure to take a screenshot of it or print it out for later reference. Keep your files chronological so that, as things develop and an outright lie is brought out in court, you have proof to counter it.

I probably repeated the following mantra to myself a thousand times while the circus was weighing on me. It gave me perspective and I know that it's true.

There are billions of people on this planet who would give a limb to have my problems, so suck it up and keep moving forward.

Chapter Seven
Takeaways and Action Items

- Separating a shared living space can be devastating. If you are the one moving, do so with as little fanfare as possible. Take only what you need from the home.

- Take pictures of any jointly owned items that you would like in the settlement. Short video records of rooms will create a useful inventory.

- If your spouse is moving out, give them the time to do it. Packing up takes time, and they may need some time alone to grieve. Be reasonable about the time you allot them.

- Do not hide or destroy anything owned by your spouse, even if you are the person that purchased the item.

- Speak to your attorney about closing jointly held credit cards and bank accounts. Be sure to keep copies of all statements and note where any funds go once an account is closed.

- Keep your journal up to date and in chronological order.

CHAPTER EIGHT

MY FIRST DAY IN COURT

All Rise.
I cannot believe I am in this courtroom; how the hell did life come to this?

Court is an intimidating place, and no matter how many times I went (it was far too many), I was as nervous as hell; the episode always took a toll on me. Prior to a hearing, there were extended meetings with my attorney, strategizing and preparing for the impending day. It was nerve-wracking; and leading up to the court date, sleep was difficult if not impossible. When you go, take a deep breath and know that it will be over quickly.

In the View of the Court

In divorce court, whenever there's a conflict, some blame is put on both parties. The court system generally views divorce as just a couple of people who can't get along because they're both *fucked up*. Regardless of the truth, you'll feel like the blame is half yours. It's not a fair system, but it is the one you are blessed with.

How your state and jurisdiction views and handles divorce is something an attorney can explain to you. I recommend that you ask your lawyer how the local courts may weigh mitigating factors in deciding on child custody, separation of assets, and child support. Where I live, judges are basically splitting everything fifty-fifty, and unless you're married to a convicted murderer or a pedophile, the outcome of custody is almost predetermined. Be mindful of how much of a fight you want—and what the end results are almost guaranteed to be. Proving infidelity or abandonment is a high hurdle; so if you go that route, be aware of the huge expense of a drawn-out divorce.

In my area, if it's determined that a spouse is at fault for the divorce because of cruelty, abandonment, drug abuse, physical or mental abuse, or adultery, assets are not always equally split. Proving these things is difficult. Each jurisdiction handles things differently; ask pointed questions about these issues so you understand what you're up against.

As I wove my way through the system, I definitely felt that there's an unfortunate bias against men. Men are not automatically seen as the nurturing parent in the way women are. I think this is slowly changing. Is there still a bias against men? In many cases, it seems so.

My First Day in Court

I had spent hours with K, discussing all the details of the breakup. He grilled me on the reasoning for the restraining order and said, should I be required to testify, I would need to be specific about dates, times, and exactly how Gigi physically attacked my daughter. Because it was the truth, I wasn't scared; but the thought of telling the court (and the world) about a family matter was truly disheartening.

Gigi hired a well-known, ruthless lawyer, Thomas Aikin. What baffled us was the fact that she had hired a criminal lawyer. The guy was famous for defending murderers and rapists; he was not known for divorce.

The courthouse wasn't a place I'd ever been, and I didn't know anything about it. It's a large, gothic building in the center of the main city, crowded with all kinds of people coming and going. My heart was beating out of my chest as I went through the metal detectors.

"Empty your pockets, please."

As I entered the main lobby there were police, lawyers, criminals in handcuffs, and a slew of people seeking divorce or custody of their kids. The restraining order was still in place, and the mother of my children was out for blood.

I met with K in the lobby just outside our courtroom for the final strategizing prior to the start of the circus. K was the pit bull of divorce lawyers, and we figured we knew pretty well what was coming our way. There must be twenty different courtrooms in the facility. Large screens in the main lobby listed all the fun for the day.

O'Brian v O'Brian Courtroom 3-C.

"Wow, my name in lights."

"All rise. The Honorable Francis Cruz Presiding."

Five or six other couples appeared on the calendar ahead of us that day, so I got to listen to their issues for thirty or forty minutes before we were called.

"Case number DM 00594-14 O'Brian v O'Brian."

K and I walked forward and sat at the plaintiff's table. I looked over to see Gigi in all her glory. I thought to myself, *Holy shit! I've never seen anyone look that mad.* She and her attorney sat at the defendant's table.

I could not have foreseen the hell that was upon me. It's probably best that I didn't know at that moment what was to come; because had I known what the following two and a half years of my life were to hold, I would have likely given up right then and there.

The defense attorney was first to speak, and my heart immediately sank into the pit of my stomach.

"Your Honor, the defense would like an immediate withdrawal of the misguided and illegal restraining order against my client and furthermore request the immediate drug testing of the plaintiff. He is an alcoholic and a habitual marijuana smoker and is a danger to his children."

Needless to say, we obviously had not anticipated *everything*. My ex's attorney was loud and assertive, and his claims drew an immediate *"I object"* from K. At that point, both attorneys were standing and yelling, and the judge was just trying to get things back in order. Because of this outburst of bravado, the judge never asked me anything about the restraining order; he was busy arguing with the two lawyers about the merits of the call to have me drug tested.

"Order! Order! Mr. Aikin, I can assure you that no one in this courtroom is getting drug tested today, and your assertion that the court should order such a thing is out of line. I hereby order Child Protective Services conduct an immediate Custody Study. The children are to remain with the plaintiff until such time that the study has been completed and we reconvene here in thirty days. Mr. and Mrs. O'Brian are to set up mediation with Dispute Resolutions, and Angel's House is to be utilized for the visitation, twice weekly."

The call to have me drug tested freaked me out. I was certainly no drug addict, but Gigi had hoped to incriminate me for smoking da kine regularly—as do millions and millions of lawyers, doctors, policemen, and yes, judges. I quit smoking weed that day and for a couple years—didn't touch it. I buried my stash in a sealed cookie jar in the back yard that afternoon. Waste not, want not.

My First Day in Court

Angel's House

The judge had ordered that Angel's House be utilized for Gigi's visitation with the kids. Angel's House is a place in my area that is used for alleged abusive parents to see their kids under the supervision of professionals. We did try to arrange a couple visitations, but each time Gigi was on a trip with Jason, or the schedule at the facility was full. I'm really glad they were full because my kids would have wanted to kill me had they been subjected to visiting their mother with an off-duty cop looking on.

Another Try at Mediation

The judge ordered another round of mediation. Our first attempt with dispute mediation was prior to me filing for divorce, so the court mandated that we go back and try again. The office manager I had met weeks prior called me the day after our court date, and I gave her several days and times I was available to start mediation again. I didn't have a lot of hope, but a little hope is better than none.

You would have imagined that, as it was a court order, Gigi would have complied. Think again.

The company was all too aware of Mrs. O'Brian's reluctance to make an appointment and stick to it. Gigi refused to commit to a date; so after many tries the mediation company wrote to the court:

"*Dear Judge Cruz,*

We are sorry to inform you that Mrs. O'Brian will not respond to our numerous requests to schedule the mediation, and we will no longer be able to offer our services to her unless the court can compel Mrs. O'Brian to give us specific times she is available for mediation.

Sincerely,

Jessica Hernandez

Dispute Mediation

SHANE O'BRIAN

Had I been the judge, I would have considered this contempt of court; but as I learned the hard way, every can like this gets kicked down the road in the U.S. judicial system.

If I were to give you one bit of advice about going to court, it would simply be this: If you can avoid it, you should.

This was my first experience with the judicial system. Courtroom TV dramas and movies do not prepare you for the reality of it. Making sense of the waste of time and money by this bureaucracy was, and still is, beyond my comprehension. There must be a better way.

New beginnings are often disguised as painful endings. —Lao Tzu

Chapter Eight
Takeaways and Action Items

- Before you go to court, ask your lawyer how the courts weigh mitigating factors in deciding on child custody, separation of assets, and child support. Take notes.

- Prepare yourself as best you can for your court appearance. Look as sharp and professional as you can, but remember that court is an intimidating place.

- Your court appearance won't last forever. In fact, it will be over more quickly than you expect. Take deep breaths when you need to.

- Generally speaking, men are not automatically seen as the nurturing parent in the way women are. Custody questions can feel like a judgment being passed. Stay strong and keep reminding yourself that you love your children. You're fighting for their happiness.

CHAPTER NINE

CHILD PROTECTIVE SERVICES CUSTODY STUDY

All children on this earth should be cared for and protected.

A custody study is something a judge will order when there is the question of who is best equipped to take care of children involved in a custody dispute. Child Protective Services (CPS) handles the custody study. They assign a person to interview everyone involved in the custody dispute, including the children. They go to the residences of the two parents or guardians to look at living conditions. CPS will require a police clearance and three character references from friends you've known for at least a few years. The person charged with overseeing the custody study will also require information about your finances, lifestyle, and habits. When they ask you if you take drugs, *just say no!*

I turned in all the paperwork CPS requested. I gave them my basic financial info and had three close friends fill out the character reference document. I chose one woman I'd known for over twenty-five years, a friend and business partner who is the godfather of my middle child, and a golf buddy I had known for twenty years who is the godfather of my youngest child. All of them are business owners and upstanding pillars in the community.

The character references questionnaire asked some basic questions: How long have you known this individual? How often do you see him? Have you seen him interact with his children? What is your opinion of him? What do you recommend for the children? These three people were all great friends, and of course their references were glowing.

I thought I had everything in perfect order until I saw my police clearance. In 1986, I was standing outside a bar where I was working, taking a break with some friends, and smoking a joint. Policemen on bikes rolled up and got us for possession. It was a misdemeanor, so I paid my $50 fine and didn't ever think of it again. Well, not until I picked up that police clearance. Shit!

In the big scheme of things it was a minor infraction, but since my ex's attorney filed paperwork saying I was a drug addict and called me out to be drug tested in my first court appearance, I did think it was a big deal. Luckily, it wasn't.

I scheduled my interview with the CPS worker who was assigned to my case. Arriving at her office building early, I was escorted to a waiting lounge. A few minutes later a couple ladies came in and greeted me with smiles and handshakes. They led the way as we walked down the hall to a small interview room.

The caseworker started out by asking me some basic questions: How long have you been married? Is there a chance at reconciliation? Why are you splitting up? How are the kids handling things? Are you or the kids currently in therapy?

This was another instance when I had to tell a stranger about my marriage, my kids, and what had brought me to this point. There I was, a grown man brought down to tears as I explained what was happening and how devastated my children and I were. While crying was not what I had planned, I'm sure my sincerity really showed.

Next up was the caseworker visiting my house and interviewing the kids. They did not want to talk to a stranger about anything, but I told them they had to. To prepare, I cleaned the house like it had never been cleaned before, did the yard work, and scheduled the meeting. The lady was a kind person, and I knew she'd do fine with the children. She arrived on time and I showed her around the house. She was impressed with the landscaping and admired my plants and the koi pond. Then we went inside, which I had scrubbed down tirelessly.

She asked in passing , "Is the house always this clean?"

My youngest sprang forth with, *"No, never!"* It was a funny moment at a very tense time in our lives.

She interviewed the kids separately, for about thirty minutes each, and left.

The report was due back to the court within thirty days of the request, but this being a government-run entity there were delays. The caseworker had a hard time getting the necessary paperwork and references from Gigi. I know that setting up the interview and home visit with her was also an issue, but it was mandated, and the caseworker did not take no for an answer.

K called and told me the custody study had been completed, and he sent me a copy to review. One thing that stood out in the study was that my ex had only two character references. One of Gigi's references was from a good friend of ours, and the other was done by someone I didn't know. I assume she was a flight attendant friend, but I had never met her nor even heard her name before. The fact she couldn't get three references was strange. It was one of those things that made me start to question Gigi's sanity.

The caseworker had interviewed Gigi and her boyfriend at their place. Some of the details of what she and Jason said were in the report. They seemed to have their future planned out and even told the woman that they wanted to bring up all five children (my three kids and Jason's two daughters) together as a *blended* family. Ironically (or not), a movie had just been released that year entitled *Blended*. It's a funny movie, but you may not want to watch it in the midst of your divorce proceedings.

In the end, the caseworker did what I'd guess she seldom, if ever, had done before. She recommended that I, the father, retain sole physical custody of the children. She noted that my daughter had told her she did not want to meet her mom's new boyfriend, and that the boys weren't keen on the idea either. She also recommended that Gigi be granted visitation rights, but her boyfriend was not to be introduced to the kids.

K was stunned at the results. A man was almost never granted sole physical custody. K had warned me that the custody study would likely recommend joint physical custody. We were all very pleasantly surprised. By *all* I mean everyone but Gigi and her love.

By the time the custody study had come out, my ex had already changed lawyers. Her second lawyer was a lady who specialized in representing women going through divorce. My attorney knew her well and was happy to be dealing with her rather than the first showboat.

I can only imagine why Gigi fired her first lawyer—or perhaps why he decided that his client (Gigi) wasn't worth his time. The stunts he had pulled in the first hearing definitely didn't go their way.

So enter the new lawyer—and guess who gets to pay to have my lawyer bring the new opposing counsel up to speed and communicate all that has happened in the first six weeks of the disaster? Yup, me. It's up to the new attorney to review all the previous court transcripts and filings, but in the end, K charged me for all email and phone call correspondences he had with Gigi's #2. I didn't complain at that time because it was part of the game and would've done no good anyway.

Moving On

During all this havoc, I was still being a father, I was also being a mother, and I was still trying to make our lives move forward with some sense of sanity. My daughter had turned 16, and although my finances were a mess, I bought her a car and was trying to sign her up for her temporary learner's permit.

The Narcissist's Playbook

When K had first told me that Judge Cruz was assigned to our case. I recognized the name because his daughter and Elisha were on the same soccer team when Elisha was seven years old. The judge was the coach of the team.

Fast forward nine years, the day before the start of my divorce proceedings. My daughter and I were in line at the Department of Motor Vehicles, and I thought I had everything I needed to get the learner's permit. I had Elisha's birth certificate and a copy of her social security card, along with my ID. Well, who do you suppose hops in line directly behind us? Yes, Judge Cruz and his daughter, who at this time was Elisha's classmate. The girls greeted each other and talked about getting their driver's licenses. I was polite and said hello and left it at that. I knew I would be in his courtroom the next morning.

As with all DMVs, the line was deadly slow, and we waited for about 45 minutes before we got in to see one of the staff. To my dismay, he told me that I had to have Elisha's passport in order to get her license. Because the area we live in has a large immigrant population, the rules for obtaining a new license are very strict. We left without applying for the permit.

The day after our first hearing, I called Gigi and let her know that I needed Elisha's passport to get her learner's permit. It was very awkward because of what had transpired in our first court appearance, but I had to try.

"Hi Gigi, I told you I was trying to get Elisha her learner's permit for her license. When I went to the DMV, they told me I have to have her current, valid passport. Can we meet up so I can get it from you? Elisha really wants this, and you know how terrible things have been for her lately."

"I don't know where her passport is. It's probably at the house, so look for it."

"Come on Gigi, you know you have the passport. Just give it to me so I can do this for Elisha."

"Fuck you, Shane! Why don't you have your fucked-up lawyer get it for you?" Click.

K asked lawyer #1 to intervene, to no avail. After the arrival of lawyer #2, he asked her to intervene—again no progress. Gigi would lie and say the passport must be in my house. My daughter would beg and cry, but Gigi would not listen.

The second court date was upon us. In reality, the battle was just starting, but it was really beginning to wear on me. K could tell that I was not in a good state.

Court Date Number Two

Although I knew that the custody study recommended that I retain sole physical custody of the kids, K told something important: "Be ready for this judge to rule that the kids will go to a fifty-fifty arrangement, he almost always does."

I was nervous as hell going back into court. Gigi was looking stunningly pissed off, as usual. She had been lobbing bombs at me for the entire six weeks between court hearings. Her boyfriend had also taken to texting and calling me. I think both he and Gigi were trying to coax me into doing or saying something they could use against me. While I really wanted to confront them both, I knew it wouldn't end well.

Our second day in court started out a lot like the first. We were fourth or fifth in line, so for a warm-up, we got to watch the arguments of people who hate each other. In addition to my case, K was representing two other people that day, so I got to see him in action with his other clients. Then the court officer called case #00594-14 O'Brian v O'Brian.

For this lovely day, Gigi had brought her boyfriend with her, and he was seated on the defendant side of the courtroom. I had never met him, but I knew what he looked like. His wife Jennifer had sent me a couple photos. I thought that having him in the courtroom was insane, but then everything Gigi was doing seemed insane to me.

The custody study was admitted into the court records, along with the fact that there was a new attorney for the defendant.

The judge had already reviewed things, and it was up to the opposing counsel to argue the merits of its findings. Once again, the opposing counsel began with a crazy statement.

"Your Honor, Mr. O'Brian lied in order to have a restraining order brought against my client. He has not followed the court order regarding Angel's House visitation, and Ms. O'Brian has not seen her children in weeks. We move for the immediate lifting of the restraining order against Ms. O'Brian and her friend, Mr. Jason Snider. We also move that Ms. O'Brian be given sole physical custody and Mr. O'Brian be granted limited visitation with the children on weekends only. We intend to prove that Mr. O'Brian is an alcoholic and abuses drugs and thus is a danger to the children."

K almost seemed amused by this and leapt up with his objections and his counter to everything that had just been said. He was quick to point out the fact that "poor Ms. O'Brian" had spent the vast majority of the previous six weeks out of state and was not available for visitation.

After a lot of back and forth, the judge ruled that, by virtue of the CPS custody study recommendations, Mr. O'Brian retained sole physical custody of the children. Mrs. O'Brian was given limited visitation, the order keeping the children away from Mr. Snider, Gigi's boyfriend, remained in full effect, and the children were not to be introduced to Mr. Snider or be near him.

K and I had discussed some of the other pressing matters prior to the hearing. I asked that he let the judge know what was going on.

"Your Honor, the plaintiff requests at this time that Mrs. O'Brian relinquish the eldest child's passport to Mr. O'Brian immediately so he can obtain the child's driver's permit."

The judge looked over at me and said, "I saw you at DMV weeks ago. What happened?"

I replied, "I need my girl's passport in order to get the permit, Your Honor, and her mother won't relinquish it to me."

Lawyer #2 chimed in, "Your Honor, the defendant does not know where the passport is, but she believes it is in the couple's residence; and she will need access to the home in order to retrieve it."

The judge was not amused. "So you're telling me that a flight attendant has lost track of her child's passport? Very well, the plaintiff is to arrange a time for Mrs. O'Brian to go to the home and retrieve the passport."

K was not done yet. "Your Honor, the plaintiff further requests that the defendant remove her belongings from the home."

"Why hasn't that been completed? Defendant is ordered to remove her belongings from the home within the next fourteen days. Plaintiff is to allow the defendant access to the home for this purpose."

I truly think that seeing the judge all those weeks prior and the obvious lying and manipulation Gigi was pulling made the judge mad—and it really worked in my favor. This was not the last time that Gigi's lie would backfire.

When it comes time for you to go to court and deal with the judges and the court setting, my advice is simple: Remain calm and remember that the proceedings are over quickly. Be prepared, and tell the truth. Do not expect that your ex will do the same. Telling the truth means you never have to go back and attempt to cover up a lie. In all the claims and counterclaims we filed, my ex would outright lie through her teeth. This was one of her downfalls and is typical of a narcissist.

I have a good friend who is a federal defense attorney, and as I was researching to write this book, he told me, "Shane, the one thing that all judges hate is when you lie to them. They have seen it all; and if they get a sense that someone is lying, they will be mad. If you lie and it's proven to be a lie, then a judge will consider it a slap in the face and will retaliate in their decision."

It was at this time that Judge Cruz also ordered that family court be scheduled so we could begin the process of deciding who pays for what and to whom. Where I live, it's a special court that handles only one thing: child support.

No man has a good enough memory to be a successful liar.
—Abraham Lincoln

Chapter Nine

Takeaways and Action Items

- Custody reviews will bring up a lot of emotions and history, and it can be unsettling. Remember everything you've learned so far about how to remain calm in tough situations.

- Remember to keep track of all the home visits and make notes about what happened.

- Make sure your calendar is always up-to-date.

- Make copies of all the forms you fill out and add those copies to your records.

- Always remember to tell the truth to the judge.

CHAPTER TEN

CHILD SUPPORT

Pray that the stormy chapters in your life are short.

The vibe in divorce court was that of hate. Family court was all about money. Adultery and the plethora of other issues that are brought out in divorce court were not part of this equation. With that said, I soon found it could be every bit as contentious as divorce court.

In most cases, the decision as to who pays what to whom is just a matter of doing the math. It's easy if you have a steady job with a consistent monthly salary and annual income. The court will look at both parents' income and the expenses for the kids. Then, based on the circumstance of where the kids are living and the income of each parent, they determine who should pay what. This is only about child support.

If you're a business owner and your income is not set in stone and instead varies month to month, it's much more difficult to determine child support. In my business, you can have great months or even years with very high income—or conversely, terrible months or years because of economic conditions. In my case, this was a very problematic issue. The lawyers used this as a means to drag out my divorce and child support proceedings far longer than they should have taken.

Early on, K advised me that I should curtail my income as much as possible. I needed to reduce my income so the court's calculations would be skewed in my favor. While I understood the concept he was trying to get across to me, I was under far too much financial pressure to stop making money. I was paying for everything, and Gigi wasn't helping in any way. I was paying for the house, Elisha's new car, private schools, martial arts, gymnastics, and attorney fees; and to top it off, teenagers eat like there's no tomorrow. I needed every penny I could make.

It was apparent that Gigi had been given similar advice. She cut her flying schedule at work down to a minimum and was spending all her time away with her pilot on exotic trips. She had her newfound freedom, and supporting the kids was not her priority.

Preparing for Family Court

The court date was set for the hearing to determine child support. K had all my financial information, but there was a lot of back-and-forth with #2 to get Gigi's latest income info. K and I met prior to the hearing to go over all the information and try to determine the best route forward. He did the calculations and made note that Gigi was no longer flying a full schedule and seemed to be trying to cut down on income, so he used our previous year's tax returns to come up with a more accurate number (Gigi and I had always filed our taxes jointly). His thinking was that a judge would be able to see through her tactics. K knew full well that the opposing counsel would be fudging the numbers as much as possible.

Back in Court

The anxiety I felt in court was always the same. It didn't matter what the subject matter was, it was the same feeling of dread every time.

Child Support

"All rise. The Honorable Judge Lynn English presiding."

The vast majority of the cases I had to listen to before our number was called were almost always men explaining to the judge why they had not paid their child support. There were questions as to why they still didn't have a job, why they were six months behind on their child support payments, and how they planned on getting caught up. The women were almost always on offense, and the men almost always on defense. It was a sad spectacle.

Judge English was a middle-aged woman, and I could tell by watching her that she had done this for far too long. She was abrupt and just wanted to get through her day. Judging from her tone, she had seen it all. And then came me. I was the atypical case, and K seemed to relish this experience. He had seen men raked over the coals for a long time, and for me to have sole physical custody was not the norm.

Our case was finally called, and we went to sit at our respective tables. There were a lot of mitigating factors that weighed on our case. The fact that we had been planning on moving to Portland and that I had given away a lot of my real estate clients was a truth that K neatly laid out for the judge. He didn't hold back going into the sordid details: Gigi was living with a married pilot, she was purposely flying fewer hours so her income was being curtailed, she was always away and unavailable to take the kids . . . Everything he said was true, but none of it had legitimately been established at that point, so #2 argued against everything that K brought up. Both attorneys had submitted a breakdown of income and how much Mrs. O'Brian should be paying.

The truth, I was buried in expenses. House, car, tuition, living, and lawyer was all adding up to one thought that kept reverberating in my mind: *"Shane you are totally screwed."*

According to K's calculations Gigi was on the hook for almost $3,000 a month. (Flight attendants can make a lot of money.) My ex's

#2 counsel was calculating it at only $900 per month. After reviewing the calculations and asking a lot of questions, the judge came to a $2K per month figure; and since it was over three months since Gigi had walked out, she already owed me $6,000. Her lawyer did her best to show how this was a complete burden on her client and requested that the figure be reduced. She went into a tirade about how the court is ruining an already traumatized woman's life. The judge was hard-core, and she stuck to the $2,000 figure. She also ordered the immediate payment of the $6,000; and a $2,000 payment was to be made to K's office by the first of each month. So I'm sure you must know what Gigi did, right? Nope! Worse.

She refused to pay anything. Really. She didn't want to give me a penny, and although the judge had ordered it, it simply wasn't going to happen. It was about this time that K started to refer to Gigi as "Cray Cray."

It wasn't long after the first hearing in front of Judge English that we found ourselves back in family court. I was getting buried in bills and having a hard time making ends meet. Judge English was livid and did not take kindly to the fact that Gigi had ignored her court order regarding child support. She was even less impressed with the barrage of excuses that #2 was offering. The judge held Gigi in contempt of court and ordered her to pay the back child support immediately and to deliver all subsequent payments in a timely manner.

This was not sufficient for K. "Your Honor, Mrs. O'Brian has shown total disregard for this court, and we are not confident that she will make timely payments. We request that the funds are garnished from her wages from this point forward."

Lawyer #2 argued against this, but the judge agreed that garnisheeing her wages was the best way forward. She also went on to tell Gigi that if she did not abide by her order again, the consequences would be severe. I remember watching it all and just thinking, *"How the hell did it all come to this?"*

Child Support

Gigi finally did make the $6,000 payment to K's office for all the unpaid child support. K sent Gigi's employer, the airline, notice of the judge's ruling and the monthly amount to be deposited, along with my bank account information. The airline began making payments of $1,000 per paycheck into my account on the first and fifteenth of each month. It was a weight off my shoulders, and I was able to breathe again.

The takeaway from this experience that may help you on your journey is this: whether it's divorce court or family court, the process is heart wrenching. If children are involved, they should be at the forefront of your efforts. Your kids deserve to be taken care of, so no matter which side you're on, take care of them. I don't want to preach to you, but it is you who brought them into this world, after all, and they deserve to be supported by both parents. You may go into debt, and you may have to budget yourself in a completely different way. It might mean that you have to cut out luxuries. This is a new life for everyone in your breaking family, and change is inevitable.

Looking back at my situation, the $2,000 seemed like a lot to some people, but the kids' tuition alone was more than that—every month. Add in all the other expenses, and it wasn't even close to half.

Going to court is a painful process that will test you. It pits you against a person who you once loved, which can make people do some really terrible things. Hearing accusations and lies about yourself will undoubtedly piss you off. Remember that it only hurts if you let it. Getting angry about things is a normal reaction. *Letting it* go is a learned response, so make the effort to add this characteristic to your personality now. It will save you a lot of grey hair.

Keep in mind that there likely will be a steady buildup of animosity between you and your ex with each hearing. Winning and coming out ahead and making your ex pay for their indiscretions is an unfortunate path that many people take. Looking back at it, I think the typical lawyer will fuel this trajectory in the fight; but try to avoid that. Look at the situation with a clear head; hopefully, if you pull back a bit and take the time to speak honestly (off the record) with your soon-to-be ex, with luck you'll be able to work things out between yourselves.

I figured out that each court appearance cost me between $1,000 and $2,000, depending on the amount of prep time that was involved. I had a total of twelve child support hearings. I don't wish this upon anyone, so avoid it if you can.

I want to take the time to remind you once again that if you let your anger get the best of you, if you threaten or cause physical harm to your ex in any way, it will come back and bite you in your ass. What you're going through is tragic. Don't make it worse on your children or yourself by losing your cool and doing something stupid—you'll end up paying for it (literally) for a very long time.

One of the most courageous decisions you'll ever make is to finally let go of what is hurting your heart and soul. —Brigitte Nicole

Chapter Ten
Takeaways and Action Items

- In all legal procedures, judges have the final say. Always treat them with respect. If things get tense, and they very well might, you want them as an ally. Or, if not an ally, at least a neutral figure. You don't want your judge to be your enemy!

- Seeing your life—and your children's lives—turned inside out and reduced to dollar amounts is heart wrenching. Make sure you're treating yourself well, talking to friends and family, and staying healthy.

- Be careful about the buildup of animosity between you and your ex. It plays into your attorney's interest of drawing out the process and extending their billing. They might not do this consciously, but it seems to happen a lot. If you can find a way to get a larger perspective on the process, it might go more smoothly for you.

CHAPTER ELEVEN

AND THEN CAME PANIC ATTACKS

It came in an instant. My vision blurred as my mind began to spin, sweat pouring down my face. I am going to die.

I never wanted to admit to myself that I was depressed. I couldn't be depressed because I had way too much to do and there were three beautiful children depending on me. Depression was not something I had time for.

Depression (Stage 4)

Of all the emotions that you endure when suffering through the loss of your marriage and family, depression is the hardest to deal with—and the most debilitating. Whether you view depression as a state of mind or an emotion, when you're going through it, all you know is that the experience is having a profound effect on your life and your ability to circumvent life's challenges.

My inability to concentrate was the biggest factor in coming to the realization that I had a problem. From the time Gigi moved out of the house and I was left to do everything with no assistance, I was drowning. Just the everyday, mundane things like dropping the kids to and from school; preparing breakfast, lunches, then dinner (I had to learn how to cook); keeping up with extracurricular activities like martial arts and gymnastics; all while trying to earn a living and stay healthy. The tasks that were once simple were seemingly impossible. As someone who was typically very sure of himself, losing my ability to concentrate was . . . chilling.

Another sign that I was in trouble? I lost twenty pounds in the first month after Gigi's departure. I attribute at least part of my weight loss to the constant stress. The constant anxiety I was feeling made me hypersensitive to everything swirling around me. It was as if my body and mind were working constantly to make sense of what my world had become; and this in turn changed the way my body was metabolizing the limited amount of food I was taking in. I tried to be conscientious of eating, but food was secondary to the myriad of other issues I was struggling with.

Lack of concentration and dramatic weight loss were the two things that signaled to Dr. Faith that she needed to monitor me, that I was at risk for clinical depression.

My short-term memory was never what I would consider great, but this was different; I couldn't remember names, dates, important meetings, why I had walked into a room, why I'd started an email . . . There were instances when I was driving and I forgot where I was going. I'd have to pull off the road and collect myself and try to remember what my destination was. My engine was not firing on all cylinders.

Some other signs of depression are muscle pain, chronic fatigue, sleeplessness, substance abuse . . . Just do an online search for "signs of depression" and you'll find a long list.

I'd always been someone who smiled all the time. I'm happy by nature. It's a known fact that the act of smiling—regardless of your actual state of mind— sends a signal to your brain that everything is okay. I was no longer smiling. On the contrary, I'd become prone to crying, which was completely alien to me, so my body was telling my brain, "Yo. Shit is not going well here."

Dealing with your emotional well-being at this unimaginably stressful time is paramount—not only to your surviving, but to thriving after the dust settles and you've moved on with your life.

I realize that the thought of moving on is probably not where you are at this point. Trust me. You'll get through this—and you *will* be able to move forward

The First Panic Attack

The day started in a typically crazy fashion in my new role as a single parent. It had been a little over a month since Gigi had left the kids and me. My life had been radically changed, and it was difficult to keep my footing on the very rough terrain where I found myself. I was highly conscious of my struggles, but I had no idea that my mind and body would rebel against me in such a sudden and absolute way.

I had just dropped the kids at school and was heading to the office when I felt my heart begin to race. My vision narrowed, and almost instantly I saw everything in tunnel vision. I didn't know what was happening to me, and it was all I could do to pull into the nearest parking lot.

My vision all but gone, my chest tight, and it felt as if I were in a vise. I couldn't catch my breath. My heart was in my throat. Sweat poured down my face. *"I am having a heart attack; I am going to die."* The thought kept running through my head.

It may have been five minutes, or it might have been twenty-five. Sense of time and space vanished.

As I attempted to slow my breathing, I considered calling 911. I blindly felt around the car to find my phone, but this seemed to make my confusion even worse. It was as if someone were screaming at me at the top of their lungs—but I couldn't hear a sound.

SHANE O'BRIAN

"I'm too young to die. This happens to other people, not me. My kids need me. Come on, Shane, you can do this; slow it down. Breathe, Shane. Breathe. You got this."

Slowly, I began to catch my breath. I was soaked with sweat; but as the blur faded, my sight returned. I looked in the rear-view mirror in disbelief. The grey-green person staring back at me was someone I'd never seen before.

This was my first of my many experiences with the terror known as a panic attack. Regardless of how "together" you *think* you are, when trapped under a mountain of pressure with no avenue to release that pressure, eventually something will give way.

Depression and panic attacks can happen to anyone, no matter how strong you once were. I was doing my best to keep my life together. Sleep was often impossible, and the basics of kids, work, and home were simply too much to handle. I had a constant feeling that I couldn't keep my head above water. I was drowning and had no way of reaching the shore. I didn't even know where the shore was—or if there was a shore anymore.

After pulling myself together that morning, I drove directly to the clinic to get checked. Having never experienced anything like this, and not being fully aware of what a panic attack even was, I needed some answers. After I checked in, a nurse did the preliminaries: height, weight, blood pressure. Then she took my blood pressure again just to confirm what she was seeing. She led me to the examination room. I waited. Nervously.

The doctor was a woman I'd never met before. She immediately noted that my blood pressure was elevated to the extreme and that I'd lost considerable weight since my last visit. She asked me what was going on.

I didn't pull any punches. I was scared, and although telling her about my family situation wasn't easy, I knew I needed help. Through tears, I told the doctor about my wife and children, my impending divorce, and my terrifying incident that morning. She was kind and patient and took the time to listen. My blood pressure was alarming, so she prescribed something to get it down to a normal level. She also made an appointment for me to see a heart specialist the following day. *A heart specialist?!*

Then she told me something I didn't expect, "Mr. O'Brian, I think you're suffering from depression. The incident this morning sounds as if you experienced a panic attack. Antidepressants may be in order."

I was floored. "I'm so busy, Doctor, and I have to take care of my kids. I think antidepressants will put me into a fog. I'm already having a hard time with concentration. Is there something you can give me that I can take in case the panic attack hits again? Something that won't make me feel like a zombie?"

"I understand your situation. I'll give you something for the panic attacks; but take it only as needed."

The life I once knew, the life I loved, was gone—and I had to deal with the fact that it was never coming back. My poor children were only fifteen, thirteen, and eight at the time and they needed a father that was fully in control, and I was dropping the ball.

If you've never experienced a panic attack, I can explain it, at least from my experience: It's like a complete meltdown of your consciousness. I'd equate it to a system overload that causes a computer—your brain—to crash.

Over the next couple years, I came to realize how fragile my mental health really was. The panic attacks would hit at any time; while I was preparing dinner, driving my car, working in my office, or dealing with the kids. The worst kind of panic attack—by far—would hit when I was sleeping. I'd wake up in terror, my chest constricted as if I were lying under a 400-pound anvil. My pillow would be soaked in sweat. The nighttime attacks were the most difficult to pull out of because I was so disoriented, having just woken up.

What to Do When a Panic Attack Hits

The first thing to do when you're hit by a panic attack is get to a quiet area if possible and take a few deep breaths. When I experienced an attack, counting my breaths as if I were meditating seemed to help. Try to think a peaceful thought. If you love the ocean, think of yourself on a beach and picture the water lapping over your feet as you stand in the cool sand. Or, if you love the woods and the snow, picture yourself hiking on your favorite trail in the silent chill. Whatever brings you a sense of peace, picture yourself there and say to yourself, "Peace." Fill your mind with a positive image; it will help you to bring yourself out of the panic.

Taking on Depression

Facing the fact that you're not superhuman and that you are depressed is a start to your recovery. You can get through this dark time. First, connect with a therapist—I mean really connect. If you don't develop an affinity, move on until you find the right fit for you. In my area, seeing a psychologist is still stigmatized; do not let that deter you. A professional can help you understand your struggles and will assist you in navigating this life event. I had two teenagers and an eight-year-old to think about. My therapist really helped me in my approach to being a single parent. It was all up to me and me alone. I could no longer turn to my wife when my daughter was crying every night or when my youngest son was suddenly failing all his classes.

Another key? *Exercise.* I cannot express to you strongly enough: exercise is medicine. The benefits of working out are well documented. Your body releases endorphins when you exercise, which helps your brain cope with your many stresses. Exercise will help you sleep better, and in turn you'll have a clearer mind. If you've never exercised, it will be hard to start in the midst of a crisis, but you should try. You don't need to go to the gym or a fitness center; just take a brisk walk for twenty to thirty minutes three or four times a week. If you live in an area near woods or a beach, get out there and be close to nature There is something profoundly therapeutic about being amongst the trees or near the ocean.

Meditation was also helpful to me. This can be a challenge for some, but it is a worthy task to attempt. Learn to slow your mind and concentrate on the present. There are hundreds of free guided meditations online. Try them out. I found that it was much easier for me to meditate while lying down and not in the seated position. It wasn't easy at first, but I kept at this worthwhile endeavor and eventually found peace.

Talking with friends and family can also be a healthy outlet. Venting your frustrations to someone who cares and is willing to listen will help you maintain your sanity. Keeping things all bottled up is truly something to avoid. If you're alone and don't have anyone to turn to, there are a plethora of online sites to explore and chats to join. Groups are available for specific situations: men going through divorce, women divorcing an abuser, and more. The point here is that help is out there. Seek out that help and live life to its fullest.

Another biggie for me: being thankful. It's easy to forget—especially when you're facing a life-changing event. Even so, be grateful for what you have—all of it. From the sunrise of a new day to the home you live in or the food in your fridge, make it a point to give thanks for the beauty that surrounds you every day.

Another thing—give something back. There is someone out there who needs you. Make it a point to seek out that individual and make their life that much brighter for having known you. Try to bring a little joy to someone who has forgotten how to smile or laugh. Breathe life into the person who may not want to live anymore. Let them know there is a reason to live. You will not have to look far to find someone in a worse state than you are in. You may have a lonely neighbor who would love to have someone to talk to now and again, and there is likely a soup kitchen or a nursing home in your area that could use a hand. Help them and you will feel better for having done it.

At this crossroad, you need to find a way to move on. You may not want a new life or a change in your circumstances, but you've got one—so make the best of it.

It does not matter how slowly you go as long as you do not stop.
—Confucius

Chapter Eleven
Takeaways and Action Items

- Men are not generally encouraged to pay attention to our mental health, but it's very important for you, your children, and the divorce process to stay as healthy as possible. Remember to exercise and meditate, or find other healthy activities that help you get through the day.

- Know the major signs of depression: weight loss, inability to concentrate, poor sleep patterns, and alcohol or drug abuse.

- Seek help if you recognize the signs of depression. Seek out a professional therapist, continue to meditate, and most importantly, stay active. Talking to friends and family abou how you're feeling, but it's important to get those bad feelings and thoughts out.

- Know the signs of panic attacks. If you experience a panic attack, get to a quiet area, put a positive image in your mind, and slow your breathing.

- Be thankful for what you do have and, if possible, give back.

CHAPTER TWELVE

EVIDENCE

When you can't tell a truth from a lie, you begin to question your own sanity.

The only one that can lead the charge in collecting evidence is you. Your lawyer won't do it for you, so don't expect them to.

Ending the divorce quickly was my goal, but I knew early on that I might not get my wish. I knew I needed to prepare for the fight and start collecting information and evidence.

How your ex's behavior and indiscretions affect the outcome of your divorce is something you'll need to discuss with your attorney. After Gigi asked me for a divorce, I took to collecting information on her boyfriend and their affair. Having Jason's wife Jennifer wholly on my side and exchanging information with her proved to be invaluable.

Although Jen and I are polar opposites in many ways, our friendship blossomed due to our common goal: the desire to protect our children and to move forward with our new lives.

If I could have ended the divorce early and saved tens of thousands of dollars in attorney fees, I would have done it in a heartbeat. It was all so unnecessary. I'm sure your story will be different, and the things you learn along the way will also be different. This is simply how I took to the task of gathering evidence.

Jen and I had many long conversations about the time leading up to our mutual marital issues. She told me that she started noticing Gigi's name on every flight her husband was flying when she checked the flight crew information. (I didn't even know you could check names of a flight crew.) Jen explained that she had caught her husband fooling around two times prior to this and that she kept a very close eye on him. She went on to tell me that she started noticing Gigi's name at least a year prior to having hard evidence of the affair.

Jen had asked Jason about the woman who seemed to be on all his flights, but he simply said it was coincidental; she was a friend but also a happily married woman with three kids.

Of course we all know that a good Christian man would never delve into anything like that.

Jen grew more and more suspicious, but it wasn't until they were on a family vacation that Jen's intuition was proven to be right. Her daughter had been playing a game on her father's phone, and the text came over at the wrong time. The little girl's game had been interrupted with "I love you and I miss you! See you soon Jay"

The girl went to her mother, not knowing what it meant and asking to re-start the game. Jen was devastated. Little did I know that this day was the beginning of the end of my marriage too.

So, getting back to the collection of evidence. Knowing what Jen had said about our spouses flying together, I asked K if we could subpoena the flight records for both Gigi and Jason. He said it was easy, so we did it. K told Gigi's #2 that we were going to contact the airline and get all the flight records for the previous 16 months. Naturally, her attorney objected to this and stated that it would cause undue stress on Gigi and Jason, that it could jeopardize their careers. K thought it was a great idea—and the fact that they objected to it only made it better.

Evidence

It's here that I want to point out a misconception that many divorcing men and women have. People think that it will be the lawyer that takes the helm in gathering evidence and making the moves necessary to win in court. They don't. It's up to you, the person who knows the underlying circumstances, who must take on the responsibility of gathering information. Your attorney can assist by subpoenaing records and information when needed.

K called me to say that the airlines had sent him the flight records. He asked if I wanted his secretary to go over the records or if I'd like to do it. Since I didn't want the cost of his staff spending hours on it, I told him to send everything to me to compile the information.

For whatever reason, the airline made it as difficult as possible to decipher the flight information. The records were not chronological, and I had to become versed in the ways the airlines showed if a flight attendant or pilot was working a flight, being paid to transit so they could work a different flight, or flying off-line on their own free time. Because it was so scrambled, I laid out a calendar and wrote in what Gigi and Jason were doing on a particular day in a particular month. When all was said and done and I looked at it, I was sickened by what I confirmed. Jennifer had been correct. Gigi and Jason had been flying every layover flight together for at least the last sixteen months. Beyond that, they'd also been flying together as non-revenue passengers to places like Hawaii, Hong Kong, and Houston. On many occasions they were seated next to each other in first class.

By this time, Jennifer was enveloped in her divorce from Jason. I gave her a copy of the calendar I had made, and she too was disgusted by the audacity of the two adulterers. The fact that her husband had been taking exotic vacations with his mistress was new information for her.

It was so blatant. I knew that everyone in the airline must have been aware of the affair. I came to the realization that some of the people who I thought were my friends had to have known what was going on. While these people were also friends with Gigi, how could they keep that information from me? I felt like the dumbest person, the most naïve idiot on the planet. Even K had a hard time believing what he saw. I thought that, with this clear evidence, they obviously had been having an affair, Gigi would relent and accept one of the resolutions we were offering—and we'd be able to end the nightmare. Relent? Not a chance.

K thought Gigi would have caved when she saw the calendar, but we were using common sense. I learned the hard way; common sense is not a narcissist thing.

I confronted Gigi with the information I had unearthed, and she instantly became enraged. She began gaslighting me and insisting that I was not seeing what I was seeing. I'll be honest—I was dumbfounded by Gigi's complete defiance and anger at the thought that I had just exposed her for what she was. K and I realized we had to prepare for the war that was coming. A war I didn't want.

My attorney went on to subpoena Gigi and Jason to give sworn testimony at his office. It was right around this time that Gigi decided to move from lawyer #2 to lawyer #3. It felt like a game show. K told me that he'd gone up against #3 more often than any other attorney in our district. Again, I was disheartened at the idea of another new face coming into the fray.

It seemed as if we were always going to a hearing for one reason or another. Gigi and her new lawyer were trying to get the court order lifted—the one keeping Jason from my children . . . while also attempting to get the child support amended. It all made me so angry. Frankly, as I wrote this, I was again angry just thinking back on it.

A Gift from an Old Friend

When I realized the affair was in the open, I started asking some of the people—ones who I thought were friends—if they had been aware of what was going on. Gigi's lifelong childhood friend, Elisha, and I had become close over the years. I'm her son's godfather, and she's my son's godmother, and we named our daughter after her. When I asked her about it, she leveled with me. She told me that Gigi had sent her photos of herself and Jason. She told me that she encouraged Gigi to stop what she was doing and to realize what she had at home. She said she begged Gigi not to throw her marriage away. Gigi didn't listen to her best friend Elisha.

I was having serious health issues and was referred to a heart specialist, which happened to be in the city where Elisha lived. I wasn't responding to the blood pressure drugs my doctor had prescribed, and there was concern I was headed for a heart attack. I went to a hospital in Elisha's hometown. It was three days of being jabbed with needles, stress tests, an MRI, an EKG . . . In the evening I'd meet up with Elisha and her family. She was Gigi's best friend, but she's also a good person with a good heart. One evening after dinner we talked about the pictures that she mentioned Gigi had sent her. I told her that Gigi and lawyer #3 were, by any means, trying to take the kids away from me. I explained that I needed the photos to end this ordeal. Elisha told me that the pictures were on her son's tablet and she didn't know where it was. In retrospect, I know she didn't want to be involved, but at the same time she felt a duty to do the right thing.

The next day I asked my godson to let me borrow his tablet so I could video chat with my kids. He instantly agreed. It took a while, but I did find the photos. The pictures made me feel nauseated. There were several pictures of Gigi and Jason cheek-to-cheek, taking selfies on the beach in Hawaii, standing in front of a bar in Hong Kong, hanging out at a pier in Houston, and poolside in swimwear with drinks in hand.

Although I was already well on my way to getting past the hurt I felt at Gigi leaving me for another man; these photos were a knife in my heart. Seeing the joy on her face as she went behind my back was just something I couldn't wrap my head around.

The best thing about these photos was that when Gigi sent them to Elisha, they had a date stamp on them. She sent them on May eighteenth and May twenty-eighth. I remember it well because on the twenty-eighth I was in Portland looking into relocating our family—at Gigi's behest.

So I had it all. I had the calendar that showed exactly what had been going on for over sixteen months as Gigi and Jason traveled the world together. I had photos of them with date stamps, clearly showing a happy couple enjoying an adulterous affair. With all that evidence against her, how could Gigi imagine that she would win a battle in court? She'd assuredly give in and just settle. No brainer, right? Not so fast.

Deposition Time

It was tough to get Gigi and Jason to agree to a deposition date. There was always an excuse, but K let them know that, if they didn't agree to a time, he would take it up with the airline and let them know that their two fine employees have been ordered to appear to give a deposition in a civil matter. They quickly found a date when they could both appear.

Prior to the deposition, I met with K, and we painstakingly reviewed questions he was to ask, along with exactly what I knew about the affair. A court recorder was hired to the tune of $300 an hour to join us.

Jason, Gigi, and lawyer #3 entered the room, and I thought to myself that Jason was a dork and Gigi looked terrible; but that was beside the point. We were there to uncover their lies. Jason was sitting four feet away from me across a conference table, and I wanted to reach across and beat the shit out of the scumbag; but I kept my composure.

Evidence

I stared at him, and not surprisingly, he never made eye contact with me.

K told Jason that he was to be sworn in, but Jason made the excuse that due to his busy schedule he hadn't had time to retain an attorney—and he wouldn't answer any questions until his attorney was present. K told him to hire counsel stat or his employer would be receiving a phone call. Jason was excused from the room. During the five minutes Jason had been in the room, his eyes never left the floor except for an occasional glance toward Gigi. He looked as if he should have had *Guilty* tattooed across his forehead.

Gigi was up next. She was sworn in with the standard, "Please raise your right hand. Do you, Gigi O'Brian, solemnly swear . . . ?"

In that moment it dawned on me that—for a lot of people—swearing to tell the truth is meaningless.

K started his questioning with the basics: name, date of birth, current address, employer, how long in the job, relationship with Shane O'Brian, length of marriage . . . It seemed to go on forever.

I was thinking, *"Yo, K. Time is money and you're wasting my money—so what the heck, get to the shit we don't know."*

Apparently it's a tactic used by attorneys to lull a victim into a sense of ease before springing some harsh shit on them. It worked. K started asking pointed questions about Gigi's relationship with Jason. When did you first meet? Are you living together currently? Are you in a sexual relationship at this time? When did the relationship start? Then he brought out the calendar I'd made containing all the flight information.

K went on to grill Gigi. The heat turned up. Did you and Mr. Jason Snider, a married man, fly together on this date? Did you fly together on this date? Did you fly together offline to Hawaii on this date? Were you seated together in first class on this date? What about this trip to Hong Kong . . . ?

Then came the bomb. K broke out the pictures that I'd gotten from Elisha's son's tablet. K had gotten the photos blown up to 8×10. Very impressive.

K dove right in. "Mrs. O'Brian, do you recall when this photo was taken? It looks as if you are on a beach in Hawaii, is that correct?"

"We are friends; and there is no law against friends going to the beach."

"Okay, Mrs. O'Brian, how about this photo? It looks as if you are traveling together in Hong Kong, perhaps; is that correct?"

"I don't remember."

"Do you remember this photo? It appears that you are at a bar in the states having a drink." He plowed on, not waiting for an answer. "Then there's this poolside photo of you two together. Do you recall these photos?"

Gigi's #3 was just watching everything unfold;, and by the look on his face, he knew they were screwed! He needed to do something, so he finally opened his mouth.

"I would like to consult with my client in private for a few moments. Let's take a fifteen-minute break."

K had no objection, and either did I. There's no way for me to explain the look on Gigi's face as she exited the conference room. It was hatred, anger, and shock—all wrapped into one ugly scowl. Gigi had no problem staring me down with that look of death.

K, the expensive court recorder, and I waited patiently. I briefly considered how much that quarter of an hour was costing me. The two came back into the room, and if I were a betting man, I'd say that Gigi's lawyer had just told his client that they were fucked.

The questioning continued for another hour or so. K was asking a lot of questions over and over, and he was playing it like we had more information that we hadn't disclosed yet . . . seemingly with an unspoken warning: *You'd better not perjure yourself.*

Evidence

During Gigi's testimony she made a huge mistake. K pushed her on the fact that she and Jason were seated next to each other on a flight that arrived late at night in Houston—and that they flew out to San Francisco together early the next morning. It was all documented in the calendar.

"Mrs. O'Brian, you have stated that you and Mr. Snider are friends. You flew to Houston seated next to each other in first class and arrived in Houston at 11:45 p.m. You then left the following morning at 6:20 a.m. to San Francisco. Where did you stay that evening? Did you stay together? You are friends, after all."

"We stayed in the airport hotel that evening then went on to San Francisco where Jason stayed with his cousin and I stayed with my brother who lives there."

"To be clear, Mrs. O'Brian, you and Mr. Snider stayed in a Houston hotel for one night together; is that correct?"

"Yes, that is correct, but we're friends, and we had separate beds."

K was not about to let it go there. He smelled blood in the water and really wanted to push the issue. I sat there listening. It was almost like an out-of-body experience. I just watched as my wife admitted to staying with a married pilot in a hotel room—and we were supposed to believe that it was a platonic relationship?

"Mrs. O'Brian, are we to believe that, after flying multiple layover flights together every month for the past 16 months, after taking several offline trips together to exotic destinations, betraying your spouse and Mr. Snider's spouse, that your relationship was nonsexual? Did you then or do you now have a sexual relationship with Mr. Snider?"

"We were friends at that time and had no sexual relationship until well after Shane filed for the divorce; and furthermore, I don't care what you believe."

"Mrs. O'Brian, I will again point out the photos of you and Mr. Snider. Do you think that these photos depict a couple of friends, or two married people who are in a sexual relationship with someone other than their spouses—in other words, a couple having an affair?"

"I told you, I do not give a shit what it looks like to you or what you believe."

Gigi's lawyer finally spoke out and made an objection to the line of questioning and the fact that K was badgering poor Ms. O'Brian. It was then that we decided to adjourn.

It had been over two hours of back and forth, two hours of Gigi staring at me with more hate than you can imagine.

It took less than two minutes from the time Gigi left the room that my friend Elisha texted me. "Shane, what is going on? Gigi just texted and called me a fucking traitor. I knew you got the photos from the tablet, but I thought you were going to leave me out of it. What happened?"

"Hi Elisha, I'll let Gigi know that I stole the pics. I don't want to get between you and Gigi. I'll try to make it right. Sorry."

"Shane, she's so mad. She said I'm a back-stabbing traitor. I don't want to be part of this."

"Elisha, I'm honestly sorry. I'll do what I can."

I told Gigi that Elisha had nothing to do with me obtaining the photos . . . and that it was her own fault for sending pictures of herself and her lover over social media. You can imagine that didn't go over very well with Gigi, and she rejected it outright. Elisha and Gigi are no longer friends. Obviously. This wasn't something I wanted in any way, but it was collateral damage. I'm still very close to Elisha and her family, and we see each other as often as possible.

What did I learn from all of this? I learned that you have to gather all the information you can. You must dig to find out what happened. If for no other reason, it will give you closure and you will lose the sense of helplessness that you feel when you first hear, "I want a divorce."

Evidence

Betrayal leaves us at a fork in the road . . . We can become stuck in a bad moment forever or we can put it behind us for good. We decide our path. —Carmen Harra

Chapter Twelve
Takeaways and Action Items

- Only you can lead the charge in collecting evidence. Your lawyer won't do it for you, or they will charge you for it, so don't expect them to.

- Your attorney is there to do what you ask. They can assist by subpoenaing records and information when needed.

- Use care and tact when reaching out to friends and connections regarding your spouse. They don't want to be forced to pick a side.

- Listen to what your friends and connections say about you. You might have some tough lessons to learn, but that knowledge will help you deal with the process. If you know how your ex views you, you can anticipate how they will try to hurt you.

CHAPTER THIRTEEN

PRAYERS UNANSWERED

There will inevitably be times in your life when that which you want the most is the worst thing that could happen.
Be careful what you pray for.

Are there people out there who will see your situation as an opportunity to take advantage of you? The unfortunate answer? Absolutely. At the lowest point in my life, my spirituality and my faith in humanity was profoundly tested.

During the divorce I prayed about many things. It was in those times that God seemed to say "No Shane, I have other plans for you." That His plan, in the end, was better than mine. The following is a true story.

Shortly after Gigi asked for the divorce, I realized we couldn't relocate to Oregon. I knew I had to cancel the sale of our home. I couldn't ask my kids to move out of the house where they had grown up.

The couple who was set to purchase my home were real estate agents who I'd done a lot of deals with, I always considered them friends. Adam and Marie were in the process of selling their condominium, and Marie was excited about moving into my house.

Once I made the decision to stay, I called them up and told them the truth—that my wife was having an affair and had asked for a divorce. I apologized but told them that, for my children's sake, I wouldn't be able to sell the house. In an effort to do the right thing, I offered to pay them $5,000 to take care of any expenses due to the cancellation. Unfortunately, they were almost done with the sale of their condo, and they had expected to move into my place within the next 60 days; so it was an inconvenience to them. But what could I do?

I was desperate to check this item off my to-do-list, so I was disheartened when Adam said they needed to consider my offer and would let me know soon. I prayed to God that he'd take this one thing off my plate. I sent the buyers a cancellation-of-contract agreement, hoping they'd simply sign it, take the money, and be done with it. A week went by. It is hard to put into words the disappointment I felt when they told me that they had their hearts set on the house and $5,000 was not going to make them whole.

I enlisted the help of my attorney friend Sam. We discussed the situation and looked at every angle of the deal to see if there was a way out. We did find a loophole in the contract, but I didn't want to use it. My hope and goal was to end it amicably.

Sam basically said that the $5,000 I had offered was extremely generous, and while the loophole we found was in no way a sure bet, he felt a judge wouldn't rule that I'd have to go forward with the sale and be forced from my home.

I prayed again, asking God to take this one problem off my plate.

Against Sam's advice, I raised the offer to $10,000 for them to sign the cancellation agreement. Again, Adam texted me and said they'd consider it—and left me hanging.

Days passed. They weren't responding, and I grew ever more impatient. I looked at my finances, checked all my accounts, even considered my retirement account; and I felt the most I could offer was $12,000. I wrote them an email to let them know that, due to my situation, this was all I could offer them. Their response floored me. I got a return email that made me realize exactly what I had to do.

Dear Shane,

While we find your offer of $12,000 compelling and have thoughtfully considered all the expenses and trouble we must endure because of your issue, we must decline the offer. Our calculations show that it will cost us in excess of $15,000 to alter our plans on the move into the home, but we will accept $15,000 and will sign the cancelation to the contract once the funds are deposited into the escrow account.

Sincerely,

Adam and Marie

When people who I thought were friends treated me like this—all the while aware of my situation—it made me want to scream. I went to Sam's office that afternoon, gave him a copy of the email chain between Adam, Marie, and me.

Essentially, the loophole I found pertained to their financing of the home purchase. The couple was to have given me a letter from the bank confirming that their loan had been approved. This is a standard thing when purchasing a home.

Sam sent them an email explaining that, because they did not send the bank loan approval letter, we consider the contract to be null and void.

The couple responded with a bank letter showing they had been approved for the loan that same afternoon.

We countered and let them know that the bank approval was due weeks prior to that day and the contract was not enforceable.

These were people I considered friends, but they couldn't have cared less about my situation. Money can make people do terrible things. We shouldn't have been surprised at what happened next. About a week later the couple emailed us, stating they'd accept the offer of $12,000.

Sam called me into his office to discuss it. "Shane, you are dealing with a couple of royal ass-wipes here. I wouldn't give them a single penny if I were you. You went way overboard by offering that much money. For them to litigate this would mean they would need to retain an attorney at $5,000 to chase after $12,000. I recommend you tell them to take a long walk off a short pier."

"Sam, I was desperate to get something—anything—done. My divorce from Gigi has turned my world upside down, and my kids are really having a hard time. How 'bout if we offer them $2,000 to go away?"

"I wouldn't offer them anything, but I will do as you say, Shane."

Sam sent them the letter offering the $2,000 with a condition: the offer was only good until 5:00 p.m. the following day, after which all offers were off the table.

The couple sent a scathing letter to Sam saying they'd be seeing me in court. The whole situation made me feel terrible, and it just added more crap to my already huge pile of shit to deal with.

About a week later, another lawyer friend called me out of the blue. He and I had played beach volleyball together in our younger days. I'd lost all contact with him except when I'd by chance see him out in the community, which was probably once every few years.

"Hey, Shane, this is Mark Fletcher. Long time no see."

"Hey, Mark, how's it goin'? You been on the beach lately?"

"I wish! I'm calling because I had a meeting with the couple who's trying to buy your house. They gave me the rundown on what happened; and after they told me everything, they gave me your name. I looked at them both square in the eye and said, 'I know Shane. He's a very good and well-respected man. There's no way I'll take your case. I just wanted to let you know they stopped by. I called Sam already and told him as well. Judging from what those two idiots said, sounds like your life is in a bit of a tailspin. When things settle down, please give me a call and let's have a beer and catch up."

"Thanks Mark, I appreciate the call and the kind words. Hopefully we can catch up soon. Cheers."

We are now past the statute of limitations for the contract. I didn't give the couple a single penny. Keep in mind that both these people are real estate agents, and it is their job to find homes for people. Trying to squeeze me for additional money was absurd.

The moral of the story? God may say no sometimes, and it might just be the best thing that could happen for you. There were several instances when God told me, "No, Shane, that's not the path we're taking today."

Maybe the best example of this is that Gigi never accepted any of the many offers I put forth. Never. I tried my best to end the drama, and I prayed every day that we'd end the insane waste of money on lawyers and court and just move on with our lives. I never got the answer I wanted, but in the end, I got a decision from the judge that was far better than the split I had continually offered to Gigi. In the end I learned that the saying "everything happens for a reason" is a real thing.

Whether you believe in God, karma, or just fate keep a good attitude, keep moving forward with good intent, keep your children your priority, keep praying and hoping the best for everyone—even your ex; and I promise, good things will happen for you.

Every day above ground is a good day! Don't forget to smile.

Chapter Thirteen
Takeaways and Action Items

- Life changes don't begin and end with your divorce. Your plans are always changing—divorce makes all changes seem sudden and difficult.

- Remember to keep recording all the things that happen. Include good things as well as bad.

- Maintain old friendships and relationships. Time with friends will help you.

- Maintain your healthy practices and stay active in your faith tradition if you have one.

CHAPTER FOURTEEN

STEALING JENNIFER'S DAUGHTERS

For forever and a day, I will never again be surprised at the human capacity for evil.

The call came late at night, and I knew it wasn't going to be good news. Jennifer's voice was trembling to the point that she was hard to understand.

"Shane, they're trying to steal my girls! I'm going crazy! What am I going to do! I can't stop crying."

"What is it Jen? Tell me what's going on."

"Jason isn't bringing the girls back to Georgia. He filed a motion today with the court there. He's trying to change jurisdiction. He's claiming I abuse the girls and that I'm mentally unfit! What the fuck am I supposed to do, Shane?"

It was the first time I'd ever heard Jen swear. She was sobbing, and I had to try to calm her down. "Send me the papers and let me look it over. Jen, you have to trust in God and know that things are going to work out."

It was usually Jen who would tell me to trust in God's plan; and in this moment, trying to convince her of the same thing wasn't going over well.

"You don't understand—they are accusing me of child abuse! They're saying that I'm unfit to be a mother! I can't get in touch with the girls. They aren't answering their phones, and the phone at the house has been disconnected. I was even blocked from contacting them on their computers."

She was hysterical—and I could understand why. We had expected something was going to happen. Jen hadn't been able to talk with the girls for days. It was August 10, nearly one year to the day since I'd filed for divorce from Gigi and eight months since Jen had filed for divorce from Jason in Georgia. Their temporary custody orders gave Jason the girls for summer vacation, and they were to be delivered back to their mother two weeks before the start of school. Jason and Gigi had waited until the day the girls were due back to file the motion and claim child abuse.

Any time child abuse is alleged, the court takes it very seriously, no matter how outlandish the claim.

This move was taken directly from the narcissist playbook. If you're unlucky enough to be dealing with a narcissist, be mindful that using the children as a weapon is standard practice.

While this situation didn't have anything to do with my divorce directly, Jen had become a great friend and confidant—and I needed to help her. Gigi and her boyfriend were behind this; and it may sound irrational, but this was one of many instances when I felt guilty for the horrific things Gigi did to Jen and her girls. I know that, in a similar way, Jen felt guilty for the sinful ways of her husband. I guess I'd equate it to how parents would feel if their child commits a heinous crime.

At the time, I had full custody of my kids; and they were set to get back to school. I was working very hard to make the money I needed to stay afloat and pay my legal fees. The fees had become burdensome, to say the least. It was all overwhelming. But I did what any good friend would do, everything I could to help Jen get her girls back; and it didn't cost me anything but time and effort. Jen had other friends in the area, from the time she was a resident, but I was best equipped to help her.

I solicited the help of my attorney friend, Sam. He agreed to take her case immediately, then got all the necessary documents and information from Jen and filed for an emergency hearing the next day. Jen also had her attorney in Georgia file for an emergency hearing there. I helped to organize everything and agreed to testify on Jen's behalf if need be.

I saw this as a cut-and-dry, straightforward no-brainer, but the court was not so quick to agree. The time for the hearing came quickly. Sam prepped me and we went to court together. He planned to call me only as a last resort. Jason and Gigi sat on the plaintiff's side of the room and I sat behind Sam in the gallery on the other side of the aisle.

Jason's lawyer was a sleazy looking young guy Sam had never run across before. He argued that Jen had stolen the children from Jason and illegally transported them across state lines for the purpose of getting them away from my town's jurisdiction. Jason's lawyer further alleged that the younger girl had shown signs of trauma and indicated her fear of returning to her mother.

Sam took to the task of pointing out the obvious. "Your Honor, this is clearly a violation of the Child Custody Protection Act. My client filed for divorce in the state of Georgia, and the plaintiff responded to that filing a full eight months ago. The minor children have lived in Georgia for the past fifteen months and attended school in Georgia the past school year. The girls were to have been returned two days ago, as per the custody agreement; and the allegation of abuse is absolutely false. At this time, I submit to the court a letter from the girls' psychologist, which clearly shows that the children are under extreme stress and that they do have issues. Those issues are related to their father, the plaintiff—specifically because the children have become aware of his extramarital affair. Georgia clearly has jurisdiction in this case, and we move that the plaintiff be ordered to return the children to Georgia immediately as ordered by the Georgia courts. My client has not been able to speak to her daughters for the past five days—and this too goes against the court order. The defendant wants immediate access to the girls via phone or Skype. The plaintiff has blocked my clients from all the children's electronic devices."

I thought to myself, *Good job Sam; we should wrap this up now.*

Right or wrong, the court will painstakingly look at every angle of an issue, especially when children and their welfare is involved.

Our hope was that the judge would rule the case jurisdiction was with Georgia because so much had already transpired there. There was proof of motions and counter motions, hearings, and court orders; but as I said, the courts never want to make quick decisions.

The judge stated he would review all the documents and confer with the judge in Georgia to determine jurisdiction. In the meantime, Jen's girls were to be interviewed by Child Protective Services (CPS) to determine if there was any abuse in the home with their mother. The judge also ordered that the girls immediately be allowed to speak with their mother with no interference. At the time, Jen's girls were six and nine years old. They were just innocent little kids being used a pawns in a sick game.

As Sam and I walked to my car that day, I saw Gigi and Jason walking out of the courthouse hand in hand with the two little girls. Gigi's mother was dragging along behind them. Those two girls had no idea the terrible thing their father and his mistress had just done. It made me sick to my stomach.

After consulting with Sam, I called Jen to give her the news. Jen was a complete wreck, and talking to her through her tears was gut wrenching. Jen loves her daughters with all her heart. She was distraught at the idea of her girls, who had been having so many issues since the separation, having to answer invasive questions from a complete stranger working for CPS.

To me, this truly was a sick move by Gigi. I didn't know who she was anymore. It was as if I'd been living in an alternate universe, emerging to find that Gigi had become a she-devil.

The ten days that followed were rough. Time seemed to have almost stopped. The days were filled with so many twists and turns, and it felt as if it would go on forever, that the end would never be found.

What transpired next was unexpected. It seemed to go against any sensible protocol.

CPS interviewed only the younger girl. Not only that, she was interviewed with her father sitting next to her. Her older sister was never asked any questions to corroborate what she was saying.

CPS reported to the court that they had found sufficient evidence that the mother had slapped the young child on several occasions. However, it did not constitute child abuse. The child had shown reservations about returning to the mother, but CPS didn't feel keeping the child from her mother was warranted.

Another move out of the narcissist playbook is to tell the children things that never occurred and remind them often of it to get them to believe that it had happened.

"Baby, remember when your mom slapped you after school? That really made me mad! I will never slap you. I'll make sure your mom doesn't slap you again! I bet it really hurt your feelings."

Yes, this is actually something a narcissist will do. It's detrimental to a child, but narcissists care only about winning and getting their way.

It was August 20; the girls were to start school in Georgia in four days. Jen and I discovered that her girls had been enrolled in the same Christian school my kids went to. Jen called the pastor, told him what was going on, and emailed him the divorce papers and custody orders. The school promptly removed the girls from the enrollment list.

The hearing in Georgia didn't go well for Jason. The judge held him in contempt of court and ordered the girls' immediate return. He also ordered that Jason pay all legal costs incurred in Georgia to litigate this motion.

The judge in my area ordered the return of the minor children to their mother. Jen got her girls back at 1 AM on August 25th. The poor kids were under so much stress they missed the first week of school. The damage to their mental states was significant. Starting school a week late after being in the middle of a legal battle between their mother and father would have been bad enough. Then they had to travel thousands of miles home to Georgia with their father and his mistress. It was too much for them to handle. Jen made arrangements for the girls to see a child psychologist as soon as time allowed. It took months of therapy to get them back on a solid footing.

This all may seem unbelievable—but these were actual events.

Jen's circumstances reminded me of the effect that a restraining order or a claim of child abuse can have on a child. When I filed the restraining order against Gigi, I truly felt that I had no other choice. Did Gigi slap Elisha on more than one occasion? Yes. Were there many instances when I had to get between Gigi and Elisha? Yes. Did I consider Gigi's slapping Elisha child abuse? No. But I did feel that, for Gigi to return to my home—my children's home—whenever her boyfriend was flying would be detrimental to their well-being and mine. I did what I felt I had to do.

There may be times when extreme measures are needed. I pray my kids never suffer from anything I've done in my efforts to protect them. My advice: Protect yourself, protect your children, but do not lie and do not take legal action lightly. It may come back to haunt you.

It takes a special kind of twisted to hurt your own child.

Chapter Fourteen

Takeaways and Action Items

- Remember that your record-keeping is part of a strategy to support and protect you. If nothing bad happens, that's great. But keeping good, clean records will help if something goes wrong.

- Children should never be used as weapons. That applies to you as well as your spouse.

- Keep in mind that the law is a powerful weapon, but it can cut both parties. It can be much simpler and easier to negotiate without involving a judge.

CHAPTER FIFTEEN

DATING AND FILLING THE VOID

The empty space next to me was a constant reminder—I am lonely.

While traversing the ins and outs of divorce, you may become lonely. Desperately lonely. Your kids fill an emotional section of your heart, as do your family and friends, but there's something missing and you may no longer feel complete. You no longer have that someone special, and it might feel as though there's a hole in your heart. I wasn't sure how to fill the hole in my heart. More importantly, I wasn't sure I wanted to fill that hole ever again. The fear of being hurt or hurting someone else was inconceivable.

Trust

When you've spent many years in a relationship and one of the pillars holding that relationship together was trust, moving on and trusting someone after being betrayed feels impossible. I still don't know if I ever want to trust someone again. Is it worth it? What if she betrays me too? I trusted my wife. I knew she would never fool around behind my back.

You get the point. Trusting again is a hurdle that, hopefully, you'll be able to overcome in time.

I read somewhere that for every five years of marriage, you need one year to overcome the pain and loss after a divorce. I am past the five-year mark since my ex walked out the door. I don't feel any pain, but I do still feel a sense of loss and distrust. The loss of my wife is not an issue, but I feel a loss of family. I know my kids still grieve about the fact that there will be no more Christmas, Halloween, or family gatherings with both their mom and dad. As for trust, I'll be straight; no matter how long I'm with someone I don't imagine I'll ever fully trust her. It's a sad truth, but a truth nonetheless.

Learning to Be Alone

From the beginning of my therapy, Dr. Faith pushed me to learn to be alone. "If you aren't happy with yourself, you can't be happy with someone else. It all starts with you, Shane. Take this opportunity to learn to be alone; and after you're comfortable with that, being with someone else becomes a lot easier. When you're happy with yourself, having someone else becomes less important, so try being happy alone."

I do not want to sugar coat this nor make light of it. While you may not be at a point that dating is important to you, it may eventually become something that you desperately want and need. Humans are social animals. We need companionship; it's in our nature.

For the most part, I had always either been in a relationship, or working hard to get into one. I enjoy female companionship; and just having someone to turn to when I'm happy or sad, confused and angry, or steadfast and joyful—having another person to share in those feelings, is something I relish. This may be a less-than-accurate analogy, but it's like when you're golfing and you hit that perfect drive or you sink the thirty-five-foot putt; having your golf partners there to cheer for that amazing feat is what it's all about. If you aren't sharing it with someone, it becomes a lot less fun.

Dating and Filling the Void

During my divorce, especially at the beginning when my duties as a father and breadwinner were so overwhelming, I simply didn't have the time or energy to put into finding someone to love. It took many months after Gigi's departure for me to be ready to even venture out of the house for any fun or excitement. I was not prepared for this part of my new life.

Dating in a New Age

We are now in the age of social media with a plethora of dating sites. In the current atmosphere, meeting in person and getting to know someone the old-fashioned way (in a bar, at a restaurant, or in some other social setting) is increasingly unlikely. The old way may not even be in your best interest to attempt. Of course, I do not purport to be an expert in this area in any way, shape, or form.

I was about to turn forty-nine when Gigi asked for a divorce—not a spring chicken by any stretch, but I wasn't dead, either. I knew about dating sites and apps, but in the town I live in, it did not seem to be popular, I looked at some of the prominent sites and quickly dismissed the idea. I saw a lot of lonely people who wanted to hook up. I guess I'm a bit old-fashioned, but that was not where I wanted to go. A chance to hold someone's hand was what I wanted. I'm not a psychologist, but many of the strange posts seemed more like cries for help to me. Just my observation.

However you move forward, do so cautiously. The dating scene and the way people interact is likely far different from when you were in high school or fresh out of college. If you're looking to date someone your own age, I imagine things will be more understandable for you. If you end up dating a much younger or older person, there will likely be a generational gap to overcome. I'd been out of the dating scene for a very long time; and as soon as I started testing the waters, I realized I didn't know what the heck I was doing.

SHANE O'BRIAN

My Experience

The bar scene in my area is different from most places in the country. I live in a place where there are a lot of military personnel. This is my nice way of saying that every place I walk into is a sausage fest. The ratio of men to women on an average night at one of the hot spots is three to one. No matter what kind of shape I was in, a forty-nine-year-old dude doesn't quite match up with a twenty-eight-year-old stud.

I had serious confidence issues, which was foreign to me. I've always been sure of myself, confident in the way I looked and acted. But I'd just been dumped. Although I was moving forward, that reality was never far from my consciousness.

There was a lot to consider: *How do I meet a woman? How old should she be? Will anyone find me attractive? What do I tell them about my situation? What do I say about my kids? What if the kids find out I'm dating? They will be devastated. I want someone, but I don't want someone. I want closeness, but I don't want closeness. I want to love, but I don't want to fall in love, and I don't want anyone to fall in love with me because I am totally NOT ready for that shit . . .* I'd often argue with my inner voice, and for a long time, I wasn't sure which direction I wanted to go. These are all normal feelings and questions for which the answers are going to come from within you and from nowhere else. Be patient.

I had more questions than answers, that's for certain. I spoke with Dr. Faith about some of my reservations, but I was not comfortable talking about dating and my anxieties regarding finding a new partner with her. So, I just did what I thought was best. I waited. And I just figured I'd cross the *relationship bridge* if and when I came to it.

You may be able to relate to these feelings, but then again maybe you can't. This was the one subject that I couldn't bring up with anyone.

Dating and Filling the Void

I wasn't comfortable talking with friends or relatives. This was highly personal, and I knew I had to work through it by myself.

When I was younger one of the rules I followed was that, if you are looking to meet a woman, you should always have a good wingman. Well, I didn't have a wingman, but I'm not sure how much it would have mattered. When I ventured out on my own, I felt awkward; so I usually retreated home within the hour.

It took a while for me to grasp the inner workings of single life again, and in actuality I'm still not very comfortable with being single. Venturing into flirting—or trying to figure out if the woman staring at me is interested or if she's thinking, *"Wow, this guy is old!"*—has taken some getting used to. I still haven't mastered it.

I was a party animal in my teens and twenties. I dated a lot of women and enjoyed every experience. By the time I got married, I was done with the crazy party life and content to be with my wife and kids. They were my life and I didn't miss going to the bars. But in this new and uncomfortable position, I was lonely.

I knew a lot of women in the gym, but from what I could tell, most were already taken; and I didn't want to come across as a weirdo, scoping women in the gym. I'm always friendly, but I'm in the gym for my health and everyone else is too. I didn't want to disturb a woman during her workout with, "Hi, I'm Shane. Are you new here?"

About six months into the divorce I started corresponding with an old friend, and we really clicked. It went from texting and talking here and there to an everyday thing. While we had never had an intimate relationship before, we really fell for each other. We were opposites. I had the wild, crazy past, and she was from an ultra-conservative family. We were *perfect* for each other. It was a long-distance relationship, which was probably for the best.

It was a joy to get to know her again. She was a great listener, and while I didn't like to talk about my ongoing divorce too much, when I was super stressed by the crazy circus, she was there for me and helped me get through another day. She gave me the hope I needed, the hope that life would return to normal. She made me feel as though I wasn't "damaged goods."

It was a long long-distance relationship, but we'd meet when we could, and the sparks flew, and life was great for those days and nights we were together. The hope that she brought to my life was precious to me. I felt a deep sense of belonging when I was with her.

Long story short, it was too much for me to handle. I knew that my priority at that time had to be my children and their well-being. I don't think she was the wrong person for me, but I do know it was the wrong time. To make a commitment, it must be the right person and the right time.

No matter how deeply I felt for her, I was determined not to break her heart. I was not going to make her miserable. I was falling in love and knew she felt the same way. In the end it was too complicated, so we broke things off. While we both felt terrible about it, we could also see the truth of the matter, which made the break up a little less heartbreaking. As of this writing, she is in a relationship—and happy. We're still friends, and I thank God for that.

After the long-distance relationship, I dated a beautiful woman who'd been divorced for about five years. She was bitter. I encouraged her to let the anger go, but I never saw her lose the hate. I stayed friends with her but didn't pursue a romantic relationship.

Eventually a friend introduced me to a really nice lady. She was a year older than I was and in great shape "for her age." I hate when people say that about me. She was divorced 18 years prior to meeting me, had three grown children, five grandchildren, a good job, a nice house, and a fun attitude. She'd given up on dating and was very content to live her life alone with her kids and grandkids—until she met me.

I was up-front with Lisa. I let her know on our first date that I was not a good bet. I explained that I was going through a very ugly divorce and it was taking a toll on me, and a long-term relationship was not in my future. I imagine this came across a bit pitifully, but she wasn't completely turned off. Our first date went on to be a lot of fun. We laughed and enjoyed each other. I got to hold her hand. That was nice.

Introducing Lisa to My Kids

After a year of seeing Lisa, I felt it was time to tell the kids I was dating again. For the most part, I had seen Lisa only when Gigi had the kids. When the kids were with me, we didn't see each other. I felt that this arrangement was unfair to her, but she never complained. I wanted to tell my kids because I thought that it was important not only to show them how relationships were supposed to progress in a *normal* way, but also that I would be okay without their mom. I was not yet officially divorced, but I was well on my way.

I thought long and hard about how to introduce the idea that "dad is dating" to my precious children. I started by telling the kids I had a date with a woman and I would be back before midnight. I began mentioning Lisa by name. I did this for a month or so. I finally told the kids that Lisa would be coming over for dinner.

It was extremely awkward for everyone, but we got through it. The kids liked Lisa and they were respectful and nice to her.

I never pushed the kids to talk about my dating with me. I never asked how they felt about it. I knew it was just something they had to accept, and I didn't want to force-feed them on the subject. Is that the right approach? I don't know, but it worked for me.

I would like to say that Lisa and I are still together and my life is complete with a new partner and beautiful relationship . . . but that would be a lie. The truth is, I began feeling scared shitless of the thought of her staying with me—and equally terrified of her leaving me. We had been together for over two years. We'd traveled together and had some fantastic times, but the relationship became so serious that I was no longer comfortable with it. I knew that the commitment to stay with Lisa forever wasn't something I could do. I began to feel bad when I was around her because I was dreading the inevitable. I knew that eventually I was going to break her heart. I thought long and hard about how to approach Lisa, how to explain my feelings and my inability to commit to her the way she deserved. I knew I had to be up front and honest and tell her face-to-face. A "Dear Jane Letter" was out of the question.

The time to level with Lisa came. It was painful to see her completely break down. My instinct was to hold her and make everything better, but I knew it would be wrong; so I said my piece, apologized for being me, and left.

Lisa was devastated and I felt terrible at what I'd done. I set out to have fun, not fall in love, and not let someone fall in love with me—but I failed. There's no way to guarantee anything when it comes to the dating game and matters of the heart. I'm simply conveying my experience here. I don't expect that many men or women will be able to relate, and some may think I'm a terrible person to be so anti-committal. I can only say that you have to follow your heart. If something doesn't feel right, then end it as quickly and as painlessly as possible.

It was several months after I broke up with Lisa that I got an email from her. I'm not sure what instigated the email, but I can't remember feeling worse about myself at any point in my life than when I read that email. It was simple, short, and direct.

"Shane, I can't stand the thought of you. You lied to me and I wish I had never met you."

I loved Lisa and will always love her in some way, and I wish nothing but the best for her. I was sincerely hurt by her words. I no longer feel comfortable with relationships for the fear I will again hurt someone as I hurt Lisa. I'm working on it, but in some ways Lisa's message probably set me back a couple years in making progress toward a long-term relationship. *Just keep moving forward Shane.*

I'm now completely alone and trying to make the best of it. I'm finishing my book, which I genuinely hope brings other people relief and some sense that things will get better, which has been a good thing. I've joined a couple dating sites if, for no other reason, so I can speak to it here. It's interesting to meet people online, but for someone my age, I just don't get it, but I'm trying.

I'm still at the point that the thought of marriage is repulsive. When I tell friends "I'm never getting married again," Their reply is always the same: "Never say never." Honestly, though, *never* is how I feel.

Transitioning to a new life and dating won't be easy, but as you move forward you will find your way. Take things slowly and don't look for love, and hopefully, love will eventually find you. It doesn't matter how old you are, what color you are, whether you're skinny or chubby, great looking or otherwise, there are very good people in the world; and I hope that the person you want will find you. In the meantime, enjoy being with yourself. Take up the hobby you've always wanted to try, learn to play that instrument, go back to school. Join a church club, a book club, a cooking club . . . Get out there and enjoy yourself, and I'm sure you'll be noticed. Smile and the world will smile back at you.

> *Until you get comfortable with being alone,*
> *you'll never know if you're choosing someone*
> *out of love or loneliness.* —Mandy Hale

Chapter Fifteen
Takeaways and Action Items

- Grieving and a sense of loss can take years to heal, and you may always feel some loss even decades after a divorce. It's ok to feel these things. However, it's not healthy to let those feelings rule your life. If you need to, find a therapist or other counselor to help you take the next step.

- You learn a lot about yourself when you're on your own. Take time post-divorce to learn to be alone. You'll be in a better place to start a new relationship later.

- When you do start dating, remember to explore the many options available both online and in real life.

- Remember to have fun! After a long time of heavy, difficult emotions, having fun can be hard. Focus on letting yourself have a good time. You'll get the hang of it soon enough!

CHAPTER SIXTEEN

THINGS CAN ALWAYS GET WORSE

It was in that moment that I remembered that the world is still spinning.

There were many times during my divorce that I felt things could not get worse, but God or fate would stop me in my tracks and let me know that things can always get worse.

About a year after I filed for divorce, my life was a constant struggle, but I was determined to make things right for my kids. In the midst of that chaos, tragedy hit.

My sister Melanie called me late one evening, "Shane, Mom had a heart attack. She's in intensive care and isn't doing well. The doctors are with her now."

Confusion and panic filled my mind, and I felt that maybe this was the thing that would finally put me over the edge. I took a deep breath and tried to collect myself.

"What? No. Tell me what's going on."

"We just got to the hospital. Mom was able to call 911, so the paramedics got to her right away. She was unconscious by the time they got in her apartment and had to perform CPR on the way to the hospital. I'll call you as soon as the doctor comes out and lets us know anything."

Thanks Mel, I'll be waiting for your call."

In an instant I was jolted back into the outside world. When you're going through a high-conflict divorce, you tend to forget about everything else that's going on, regardless of how engaged you might have been prior to your current circumstance.

My sister called me back to let me know that our mother had major blockage in her arteries, was on a respirator, and would remain in intensive care until she was well enough for them to perform bypass surgery. She was eighty-two and looking at quadruple bypass. We were all worried about her chances for survival.

I'm relaying this story to you because what happened next was something that I could never have imagined.

Early on, Gigi took away the free flight benefits that I had enjoyed for over twenty years. That was not a hard pill to swallow, and I had already become accustomed to paying for flights. With that said, my children still had the benefit of flying for free.

As I look back, I know my expectations of how Gigi would act and respond to this was way off. I expected her to act as if she were still a part of my family. I expected Gigi to have some compassion for our kids' grandmother. I could not have been more wrong.

I sent Gigi an email and let her know that my mom was in intensive care. I told her that the prognosis wasn't good and they'd be operating as soon as she was well enough to withstand the surgery. I explained that I wanted to take the kids to see their grandmother, as this may be their last chance to see her. This would mean they'd miss over a week of school. I also asked that Gigi allow the kids to fly using their flight benefits. It wouldn't have cost her anything—and would have saved me thousands of dollars. I am pretty sure, by now, you can guess what Gigi did. Nope. Worse.

Gigi wrote me back and said that under no circumstances would she allow the kids to be taken out of school. Furthermore, she'd never allow them to use their flight benefits if they were traveling with me.

Things Can Always Get Worse

My heart sank. I thought that at least in this case Gigi would act differently. This wasn't about me, it was my mother, a woman who Gigi had known for over twenty years and called "Mom." It wasn't about our divorce, but I guess she didn't see it that way. Anything that had to do with me was simply a matter of hate. She never even said anything about my mother. There was no, "Sorry to hear about your mom. I hope she gets well soon."

I didn't have the time to argue with Gigi. I bought my ticket, arranged for the kids to be taken care of while I was away, and flew out as soon as I could. Gigi made everything as difficult as she possibly could. She refused to change her schedule to assist in getting the kids to and from school. She made life nightmarish for the friends from whom I'd enlisted help by badgering them about how they were caring for the kids.

My mom did go through bypass surgery several days after my sister's call. I was able to see her before she went into surgery and was there alongside her for several days after the surgery. It was a rough time for her, but I'm happy to report that she did make a full recovery.

This was just one more time that Gigi showed a complete lack of empathy and how undeniably evil she could be. This was one more case that I had trouble reconciling the wife I'd once loved with the person who was occupying her body. There were countless instances that I felt this way. My new alternate reality was *Twilight Zone* Gigi.

> *Love doesn't die a natural death.*
> *Love has to be killed,*
> *Either by neglect or narcissism.*
> —Frank Salvato

Chapter Sixteen

Takeaways and Action Items

- Life keeps happening when you're going through divorce. There will be other shocks and crises.

- Keep doing the things that keep you healthy and strong.

- Your spouse may not be on your team any more. They might be willing to help, but you can't count on it. It's hard to do, but you need to prepare yourself for the moment when they won't help you in a crisis.

CHAPTER SEVENTEEN

TRIAL

Nothing has or should have prepared you for this moment in time. The important thing to remember is that this is a moment in time.

The date was set. Wednesday, December 7, at 10:00 AM in courtroom 3C, *O'Brian v O'Brian*.

Leading up to the trial date, things were as bad as they could possibly get. Gigi had been telling my daughter terrible things about me and was obviously encouraging her to be disrespectful. Gigi told her lawyer that I was abusing Elisha and he in turn emailed K to say they'd be filing papers citing the child abuse. Gigi was seeking sole custody. Then the call came. It was around 4:00 PM Friday, December 2.

True story:

"This is Officer Sanchez from the Northern Precinct. Is this Shane O'Brian?"

"Yes, it is, Officer. What can I do for you?"

"We have a complaint from Ms. Gigi O'Brian concerning an incident from November of this year that we need to speak with you about."

"What is the incident you are talking about, Officer?"

"Ms. O'Brian has filed a complaint against you for unlawful physical restraint. She stated that she went to your residence on November 3 and you would not allow her to leave and you grabbed her and pushed her against the car, bruising her arms."

"Sir, I have no idea what you're talking about. We're going through a divorce, and the trial is set for next Wednesday. My ex has lied and told her lawyer that I've been abusing my daughter, but this is the first I've heard that I am abusing her also. It's a total fabrication. I'll come down with my lawyer on Monday to answer any questions you may have."

"No sir, you need to come down now for questioning. If you don't come down to the precinct, we'll send a unit to your home to question you there."

"With all due respect, sir, I've done nothing wrong and I need to consult with my attorney."

"Sir, what you need to do is come down and answer our questions. If you don't, we'll be sending a unit to your home."

The policeman was not taking no for an answer, and he was sounding more and more upset with me. My heart was racing, and I figured I would buy a little time and call up K.

"Okay, I will come down, but this is just bullshit."

I got off the phone with the policeman and immediately called K. It was a Friday evening, and judging from the background noise, he was already out enjoying happy hour.

"Hi K, sorry to bother you, but I just got a call from a policeman. He said that Gigi had filed a complaint that I restrained her and held her captive last month. I don't even know what the hell she is talking about. The guy asked that I come to the Northern Precinct to answer questions and give a statement."

"Shane, under no circumstances are you going to go to that police station! They'll throw you in jail and you will sit there until Monday morning when you can see a judge who'll set bail for you. Do not go in!"

Trial

"K, I didn't do anything wrong. Why the hell would they throw me in jail? They said I just need to go in and answer a few questions; then I can go."

"Listen, Shane, you do whatever you want, but don't blame me and don't call me from jail asking me to get you out this weekend—because it will be impossible. I have seen this a hundred times. The cops will *definitely* throw you in jail. They have to when domestic violence is charged."

"They said if I don't go in, they'll send a unit to my house."

"Where are the kids?"

"They're with Gigi for the weekend."

"Leave the house now. Go stay with a friend. If the police do come over, don't answer the door, don't let them into your home, and under no circumstances should you go outside your home. They can't take you in unless you're outside the house or you do something totally stupid like going to the police station. Trust me."

I called Lisa (we were still together at that point) and asked her if she would mind if I stayed at her house that night. I packed a few things as fast as I could and hit the road. I have no idea if the police went to my house that evening or not. I can tell you that I was scared shitless. Once I got to Lisa's home, I asked her to move her car so I could hide mine in her garage. After that, I felt relatively safe.

I never heard from the police again.

This is such an important lesson; and if you're going through a high-conflict divorce, you need to know in advance that this kind of tactic is likely to be utilized by your estranged spouse.

Anytime the police call you and tell you to go in for questioning, regardless of the facts they can throw you in jail. If a woman alleges that you abused or in any way restrained her against her will, the police do not need any evidence to toss you in jail for the weekend. The police can ask you to go with them for questioning, but without a warrant they cannot go into your home unless you agree to it. I guess the number one rule is don't be dumb enough to go into their lair for questioning. If you do, you are basically screwed.

I had an eye on my rear-view mirror for days after that phone call with constant anxiety just thinking of being thrown in jail. It was not a great weekend for me.

Our Last Face-to-Face Talk

On Monday, December 5, my daughter had dental surgery. Her wisdom teeth were impacted and needed to be removed before they made her straightened teeth crooked again. I had to go and pay my half of the bill. Gigi was there in the waiting room. I paid the bill and went to sit next to her. This would prove to be the last time I ever spoke directly to her.

"Gigi, I know this has been a terrible experience for everyone. I don't care about any of the past. I don't care that you filed false charges against me and tried to get me arrested. I honestly do not care about any of it. You have decided to move on with your life without me—I got that. A trial will cost an additional $10,000—and that's just my lawyer's estimation on his fees. This is the kid's money. Let's just agree to split things fifty-fifty and move on with our lives."

"You're insane, Shane! Do not talk to me and stay the hell away from me. You're an idiot; and once you're exposed to the judge, I'll get back my house and my life—so fuck off!"

My heart sank. I felt profound sadness in that moment—so much so that I truly wanted to cry. Tears welled up in my eyes as I looked at Gigi and was again struck by the fact that I didn't know who she was. I didn't recognize the person looking back at me. It was all I could do to walk away. On some level it was then that I realized the end of family was unavoidable. As I began to walk away, I turned to Gigi and said, "Gigi, I forgive you for what you've done, but I can't forgive you for what you're doing."

I know now that trying to reason with a narcissist is useless, but I had to try. Looking back at it, I know it was a waste of breath. If I had to do it again, I don't think I could change anything. I was fighting for my kids. Who wouldn't do that?

Trial

Although K said he thought the trial would last only one day, the opposing counsel did his very best to stretch things out so it lasted a full two days. There were only three people slated to testify: Gigi, her sister Stacy, and me.

We were up first. K called me to the witness stand and I was sworn in. No Bible, just "Raise your right hand and repeat after me."

As I took my seat on the witness stand, it dawned on me how different the view was from this chair. The judge in his black robe sitting a few feet away. A stern-looking bailiff stood next to His Honor, and near the judge's chamber door a pretty court recorder sat ready to forever document the day's proceedings. I looked out at Gigi and her lawyer staring at me as if I were a caged animal. I'd been on the stand several times prior to this, but it was never easy. I was suddenly front and center with the entire room looking at me, waiting for me to screw up. Not fun.

K got the ball rolling by asking all the standard mundane questions: "Please state your full name and date of birth . . . Where were you born? . . . How many brothers and sisters do you have? . . . Where do they live? . . . Are your parents living or deceased? . . . Where do they live now?"

He then asked me about how I got to this point in my life: past work history, special skills, how much money I make . . . We finally got to questions concerning my meeting and dating Gigi—and eventually, our marriage.

I told the court how and where we met, what our life together was like in the early years. Then I went on to the time that we started having children. It was more than twenty years of marriage, so there was a lot to cover. It was about this time that we recessed for lunch. For me, everything that morning had seemed rather pointless. It wasn't until after lunch that we got into the meat of the bench trial. I learned that it's called a bench trial because there's no jury. Instead, the one person sitting on the bench, the judge, decides everything.

Back in my seat front and center, I was reminded that I was still under oath.

K continued, "Your Honor, we submit Exhibit A. This is information that was compiled from subpoenaed records we received from the defendant's workplace. The information is in the form of a calendar and shows where and when the defendant and Mr. Jason Snider were flying together. At the bottom of each month, there is a summary of that month's flights. We intend to show that Ms. O'Brian and Mr. Snider had been having an affair during the couple's marriage, which culminated in Ms. O'Brian eventually asking Mr. O'Brian for a divorce."

K gave copies of the calendar I'd made to opposing counsel and the judge. He then asked me about the process of compiling the information, and he even asked how I felt when I saw the calendar in its entirety. I explained that I was devastated, not only by the story the calendar told prior to Gigi asking me for a divorce, but also what it showed immediately after she left the kids and me. Her priority was Jason and traveling the world while I was left to be the lone parent. The calendar made it obvious to everyone what Gigi's priorities were.

Gigi's #3 jumped right in, "Your Honor the defense objects to this exhibit. Mrs. O'Brian and Mr. Snider are co-workers, and the calendar is misleading."

"Your Honor, if the defense counsel is suggesting that their schedule is a coincidence, I would like to point out that there are over 400 flight attendants in this base and more than forty co-pilots. This calendar

Trial

shows an obvious pattern of behavior far outside the norm. This is not a couple of co-workers who just happened to get the same schedule; and to suggest that is ludicrous."

"The defense objection is noted. The court will decide what is relevant and what is not, the objection is overruled."

K went on to ask me what the calendar showed.

I started my summation. "In January 2014, Gigi had twelve flights, and of those flights Mr. Snider was on eight of them, and they laid over together for four nights. In February, Gigi had eight flights, and she flew with Mr. Snider on six of those flights. In that same month, Gigi and Mr. Snider flew to Hawaii as non-revenue passengers, and they were there for two nights together. Then they flew to San Francisco and were seated next to each other in first class, seats 3A and 3B. In March . . ." It was a long explanation. Sixteen months' worth.

Then we submitted the photos I got from my godson's tablet into evidence. There were also some photos of Gigi walking in and out of Jason's house. Jason's wife Jennifer had gotten those from a friend who lived in the neighborhood and saw a strange woman coming and going just after Jen had decided to stay in Georgia with the girls.

"Your Honor, the plaintiff would like to submit the following photos into evidence: These are to be Exhibits B, C, D, E, F, and G. Please note the date stamps on the photos, which coincides with dates shown on the calendar when Mr. Snider was traveling with Mrs. O'Brian. The photos show the two in cheek-to-cheek poses, which is typical of a loving couple."

Objections flew and back and forth, but everything was admitted into evidence, and the process was moving in the right direction.

It was about 2:00 p.m. when K handed me off to #3.

So, #3 started out by asking some basic questions. He then went into my use of marijuana and my drinking.

"Mr. O'Brian, isn't it a fact that during your marriage you were a habitual marijuana smoker?"

"No, sir."

"So you deny smoking marijuana during your twenty-year marriage?"

"No, I didn't say that."

"Do you smoke marijuana on a regular basis now or were you a habitual marijuana smoker during your marriage?"

"I smoked weed occasionally but have not smoked in a very long time and am happy to submit to a drug test anytime."

K felt the need to chime in and put #3 in his place. "Objection, Your Honor. Mr. O'Brian has maintained that he has smoked marijuana in the past but has consistently offered himself up for drug testing. The defense counsel never saw fit to have him tested, only to now, at trial, again bring up something that has never been established."

"Objection sustained. Please move on in your questioning."

"Mr. O'Brian, are you a habitual drinker, often finishing a bottle of rum in one night?"

"No, that is not correct. I have never been arrested for DUI or had any trouble with alcohol. Do I drink? Yes. Is it a problem? No."

I could see frustration growing on #3's face. He moved on to my income and taxes and why I had so many deductions, and why I was making far less money that year than in previous years. I explained that my income was hurt by the fact that I had given away clients because my wife had led me to believe that we would be moving. However, she had failed to tell me about her affair; thus, I was working to rebuild my business. Lawyer #3 was setting himself up for some really bad answers.

Gigi's lawyer then went on to ask me questions about my marriage to Ms. O'Brian. They were leading questions about how bad the marriage was and how I was not attentive to poor Ms. O'Brian—to the point that she likely needed to seek companionship elsewhere. *I was such a horrible person; she had every right to screw a married pilot.*

Trial

He didn't say it in so many words, but he was leaning that direction, and K had to object many times.

I was ready for anything #3 threw at me; and while he tried to twist things around, I just untwisted them back into place. I got into a couple heated exchanges with him, but I held my own; and after all that was said, I felt confident. There were a couple of times that I did well up and had a tear in my eye, especially when I was talking about my kids.

Finally, #3 finished his questioning, and the judge excused me from the witness stand. I went back and took my seat next to K. He leaned over to me and said, "Shane, you hit it out of the park."

It was still relatively early in the afternoon; K gave the floor to Gigi's lawyer, as he had no other witnesses. First, #3 called Gigi's sister, Stacy, to the stand.

"Your Honor, the defense calls Mrs. Stacy Yates to the stand."

"Please state your name . . . "

It was another thirty minutes wasted. I have no idea why the date my ex sister-in-law moved to the area was relevant, but Gigi's lawyer was doing his best to make some easy money.

The defense counsel finally started asking pertinent questions about when and where Stacy had first met Jason, how many times she had met him. Stacy is personable, but not a good liar.

After #3 was done wasting time, K got his chance at her—and he had made note of every misstep she'd taken. He asked her very pointed questions about whether Stacy knew of the affair, when she became aware of the affair, how many times she had met Jason prior to Shane's filing for divorce . . . I won't get into her testimony in too much detail, but there was a point in the trial that simply amazed me.

Stacy was not forthcoming, and K was getting frustrated with her because it was never a *yes* or *no*, it was always, "Well, I'm not sure if I remember that too clearly. I think I remember that, but to be honest I'm not really sure."

SHANE O'BRIAN

True story:

After about thirty minutes of listening to Stacy give half-truths and no definitive answers, the judge stopped the proceedings.

"I would like to go off the record for a moment. The court recorder is to take a momentary break."

At that point I was intensely frustrated by the way a person who I had once cared for, my sister-in-law, was lying about me to make her sister look good to the court.

The Judge continued, "Mrs. Yates, I would like to remind you of something."

"Oh, that I have to tell the truth?"

"No, Mrs. Yates, that you have to tell the truth, the *whole truth*, and *nothing but the truth*. Please answer the attorney's questions."

I am not sure if K had ever seen that before, but we both looked at each other like, *wow what just happened there?*

Stacy proved to be a pretty useless witness for the defense. Why the attorney put her on the stand unprepared is beyond me, but I was never impressed with #3.

Gigi was up next. It was getting late in the day, but the judge was on a mission to finish this fiasco, so although it was 4 PM the judge wanted to keep things rolling.

Next, #3 called Gigi to the stand. She was sworn in, but I knew that swearing to tell the truth meant nothing to her. I was prepared to hear her lie, and she did not disappoint. The attorney started with all the typical questions to eat up some time, but he finally did make it to asking her about our marriage. Gigi made our marriage sound like hell on earth. I expected as much, but when she was actually speaking, it was hard to listen.

"Shane was always stoned. He smoked weed every day and drank himself to sleep most nights . . . It was all Shane's idea to move to Portland. I never wanted to go, and my kids weren't happy about it either . . . Shane made all the decisions in the marriage with no regard for what the rest of the family wanted."

As if it wasn't bad enough, it was here that things got crazy ugly.

During my testimony, K had asked about our sex life. I testified that Gigi decided to have an IUD inserted so she didn't get pregnant again. I also noted that it was strange because it was at that time that our sex life became non-existent.

"Ms. O'Brian, the plaintiff testified about your decision for birth control. Do you recall why you decided on an IUD?"

"We didn't want any more kids. Shane was having trouble performing in the bedroom, so we were worried a vasectomy would make things worse. Instead, I decided to have an IUD inserted."

Her testimony was worse than I ever imagined. I was freaked out, and I think with every new lie, I slumped more and more in my chair. The "trouble performing" line just about put me over the edge.

It was 5 PM and time to wrap things up. Lawyer #3 had nearly finished his questioning of Gigi, so the judge said we would adjourn until December 13 at 10 AM.

But #3 jumped up and made a motion. "Your Honor, the defense requests that the marriage be dissolved due to irreconcilable differences today so my client can move on with her life."

K rose and quickly pointed out the obvious: "Your Honor, the plaintiff rejects this motion. I have not even been given a chance to ask Mrs. O'Brian one question. We are fine with reconvening here on December 13."

I was so hopeful that the trial would be done on that day. When it became apparent that it wasn't going to happen, I was disheartened. On the other hand, I knew there was a light at the end of the tunnel, and I was walking toward that light.

Trial Day Two

Gigi had her full entourage for the second day of the trial. Stacy was back and looking dejected. Jason was in the stands along with Gigi's mother, brother, sister-in-law, and a couple of her cousins.

I had no family in the area and wouldn't have brought them along, even if they lived next to the courthouse. I looked at the crowd and just shook my head. Their presence made me feel abandoned and betrayed. I guess it's all part of the deal that is divorce.

Gigi was reminded that she was still under oath, and she took her place next to the judge.

Not surprisingly, #3 killed some more time that morning with softball questions that he had obviously rehearsed with Gigi. It was almost noon; the defense rested, and we adjourned for lunch.

After lunch, it was K's turn and I think *pit bull* is the best description I have for how he acted. He immediately started asking very pointed questions. He had ammunition in his arsenal and was ready to use it.

"Ms. O'Brian, please look at the calendar dated January 2014 . . . Now please review February 2014 . . . March . . . April . . . Would you say that to travel so many trips together with any one co-pilot is extremely out of the ordinary?"

"No! I flew the flights that I wanted to fly, and it's a coincidence that we were on many of the same flights."

"Isn't it a fact you told Shane that due to new airline policy you had to fly layovers; but in fact your seniority allowed you to choose any flight you wanted?"

"I never told Shane anything like that. I flew the trips I liked to fly, period."

Gigi's big mistake came when K asked about the night she spent with Jason in Houston. She had admitted in the deposition to staying together in the hotel. K was very quick to point out that she had testified under oath, admitting to the tryst. But Gigi (not being the sharpest tool in the shed) would not relent. She tried to say that she had misspoken. K took out a copy of the deposition and read Gigi's own words aloud for the entire room to hear. He then asked the Judge to consider her testimony as perjury. The judge said he would consider it in deliberation and asked K to move on in his questioning.

Trial

Gigi was adamant that I was a drug addict and a drunk. While she was saying all of those hateful lies, I just stared at her family. Not one of them would make eye contact with me.

K went on to ask about the type of father I had been to the children. "Mrs. O'Brian you have testified that Shane is an alcoholic and habitual marijuana smoker; how was he as a father to the children?"

"Shane spent most of his time working; and when he was home, he generally stayed in front of his computer and drank. He was not what I would consider a good father."

It was at this time that K submitted into evidence a Father's Day card that Gigi had given me the year before she asked me for the divorce. There was a handwritten note from her: "Dear Shane, thank you for being the best father in the world! The rug-rats love you so much and are so lucky to have a dad like you. Love Gigi".

K handed the card to Gigi and confirmed that the note was her handwriting. Then he asked that she read it out loud. Her reading it seemed to suck the air out of the entire room. Hearing her speak those words and thinking of my kids made me cry. I realized at that moment how much my children were losing. They still had me, but they no longer had a family.

During all this, #3 would throw in objections as to the relevance of a question or the accusation that K was badgering the witness. Under the pressure, Gigi finally broke down crying. We had to stop the hearing so she could collect herself. The judge ordered a fifteen-minute break.

As I think of that day in the courtroom, it was the only time during our divorce that I ever saw Gigi actually cry. There were so many incidents of terrible things happening to the kids. Troubles in school and troubles at home left my children and me complete wrecks, but during all of that, Gigi never cried. It was only when she was forced to tell the truth or have her lie thrown in her face that she finally broke down. The fact that she had so many family members there to see the carnage was something that any normal person would regret. I doubt it even dawned on her.

After returning from the recess, K went back at it with a vengeance. The lies Gigi was telling seemed more obvious than ever. She became combative, and it got ugly. I glanced over at the crowd on the defense side of the room. There were tears in some eyes and the look of shock on many of their faces. Jason maintained his smug, arrogant look throughout the proceedings.

Thankfully, K finally said, "No more questions, Your Honor. I think that's enough,"

The takeaway here is to be prepared. Collect the evidence that's out there. It won't be easy, and your lawyer will not be the one to figure out what needs to be done. It's you who must guide the preparation for the hearings and trial. You have to figure out the best way to expose your ex for who and what they are. You must note all the problems you had during your marriage and also what was happening during your divorce process.

You have to keep records of emails and texts that your ex and or their paramour has sent you. Keep records of when your ex didn't show up to pick up the kids as scheduled, dropped them off six hours late, or failed to take them to their therapist appointment . . . and all other pertinent information. Your lawyer won't do it for you.

Believe in yourself and all that you are.
Know that there is something inside you that is
greater than any obstacle. —Christian D. Larson

Chapter Seventeen

Takeaways and Action Items

- Try to prepare yourself for extreme tactics. Rely on your lawyer and counselor for advice. You need experts to help you.

- Stay honest in front of the court. Honesty can be hard—you might want to make yourself look better and your spouse look worse—but it's the only way through.

- Hope and pray that you never have to deal with extreme tactics!

CHAPTER EIGHTEEN

THE LAST HEARING

Even when you can't see it, just remembering that there's a light at the end of the tunnel will keep you on the path toward that light.

With the trial done, the kids were splitting time evenly between Gigi's home and mine. The judge's ruling granting the divorce was still pending. One of the final hurdles still needed to be negotiated: figuring out child support.

During the two-plus years while I had sole physical custody of the kids, I was the one paying for the kid's tuition, which came to about $22,000 annually. Since custody was split fifty-fifty, all I really wanted was for Gigi to pay half the tuition. Gigi wouldn't agree to any such thing, and #3 kept the fight going by saying that Gigi had been paying too much ever since our first child-support hearing. He argued that she needed to be refunded for all her overpayments. They reasoned that since I was by then making more money, I alone should pay the tuition.

We had gone before Judge English eight times before she was promoted out of the family court circuit. K argued that because I had offered testimony before her on several occasions, she was the only judge who could properly adjudicate the final decision. That argument was overlooked, and we were passed onto another judge. It was like starting over. My frustration level with the judicial system grew even more extreme.

The first hearing with the new judge was a matter of just getting him up to speed on everything. We were back to arguing about how much I should be making, why I had so many write-offs on my tax return, why I was hiding money . . . The new judge was a rookie, and all of this seemed to be over his head.

For the second hearing in front of the rookie judge (tenth overall in family court), both lawyers were to have turned in a worksheet explaining in detail income along with any expenses that were being paid, and who was paying them. K had done his job and turned in his worksheet; and while it was not technically his responsibility, he didn't make a point of ensuring that #3 had done the same. Gigi's lawyer had failed to turn in the worksheet—so the hearing went nowhere.

The third hearing with the new judge was scheduled, and about a month later we were back in court. I was incensed about the continued waste of my kids' money and the fact that K could not end the circus. Before the hearing, I told K that if we did not come to some sort of agreement and end it that day, I wanted to address the court. K argued with me about it, but I insisted. I wanted to speak my piece directly to the court, regardless of what he thought.

The bailiff called our number, and almost immediately my heart sank. The rookie judge noted that because testimony was given in front of Judge English, he would need to review the court transcripts. This was something that had already been brought up, but I guess he didn't get the memo. I just shook my head in disbelief.

I told K prior to the hearing that I did not want to rework the numbers again. I did not want him to ask for updated income information, and if #3 asked for it, he was to refuse.

The Last Hearing

The judge was moving quickly, as there were another dozen couples who needed to argue their cases before him. I nudged K and told him I wanted to address the court. K ignored me and instead did the exact opposite of what I had told him prior to the hearing. He asked for updated financial information. The judge agreed and ordered that all income information be updated and submitted to the courts before the next hearing, which was scheduled one month later.

I was fuming. In that moment, I wanted to kill K. He had another two clients to deal with that morning, so he was not leaving the courtroom. I told him I wanted a word in the lobby, but he would only go as far as the chamber door.

"K, what the hell was that? I told you *no new numbers*—and I also said I wanted to address the court. *I am paying you to do your job.* What you have done is totally unacceptable."

"Listen, Shane, I am the professional; and what you want is stupid and could end very poorly for you, so I am trying to save your ass. This shit happens all the time, so live with it."

I was about as mad as I had ever been in my life. I emailed K and told him in no uncertain terms that he'd messed up by not following my directions. I reminded him that I am the one paying *him*, and that he needed to listen to and follow my requests. I let him know how furious I was and that the next hearing was going to be very different.

The date came for the twelfth hearing I had in family court. I showed up and looked for my name in lights on the court calendar board. I couldn't find it on the new Judge's schedule. I was baffled. K saw me in the lobby and asked that I follow him. We went to an area in the courthouse where I had never been.

K sat me down and said something that threw me over the top. "Shane, we're back in front of Judge English. The other judge felt that because we had offered so much testimony already, Judge English is the only person who can handle this case. Judge English is no longer handling family court, but she agreed to hear this one out until the end."

"Are you fucking kidding me, K? I've had it, dude. I am addressing the court today. And if you try to stop me, I'll be finding a new lawyer—and I will take this to the *ethic's board*."

At that point I was so mad I was shaking. K told me I needed to calm down and he would do his best to end it, but he also mentioned that #3 had not turned in the paperwork the judge had ordered.

Well, #3 was in the same sitting area we were, and he heard me go off. "K, fuck this! I am not going to waste any more money on this bullshit. If #3 isn't ready, then it is he who needs to pay your fee. He should be on the hook for the past six hearings. I am absolutely not going to keep paying because that asshole didn't do his job."

"Shane, you need to lower your voice and calm the hell down. I am not his babysitter, and there is no chance a judge will rule that a lawyer needs to pay another lawyer's fees. Listen man, I will do my best to end it, but I can't promise anything."

"Listen K, I don't give a shit what you say. I will end this today unless you finally do your job. I am talking to the judge with or without your blessing."

I looked over at #3 and glared at the guy. He could see what was going on and I could tell he wanted nothing to do with me.

We were called into a courtroom I'd never seen. We were the only hearing that day for Judge English. Gigi was not in attendance. To start, #3 told the court that his client was out of town and unavailable. For someone who didn't think he could possibly get madder, *I got madder*.

K was feeling my vibe and he knew he had to do his job and call out #3.

I was shaking with anger as K got things started.

"Your Honor, this is the twelfth hearing on child support, and I must tell you that I have an enraged client. We have done everything possible to end this in an amicable way, but the opposing counsel and his client have been completely combative in our negotiations to the point that they do not even offer a counter proposal to anything we've offered. The opposing counsel was to have turned in his rebuttal ordered by the court weeks ago but has not yet turned in his calculations concerning child support."

Of course, #3 quickly chimed in, "Your Honor, I have the calculations with me and offer them into court records at this time."

He handed the bailiff two copies of his bullshit arithmetic. The bailiff handed one copy to K and one to the judge.

K responded, "Your Honor, it is the opinion of my client, as well as myself, that the opposing counsel has neglected his duties on several occasions during these proceedings. We further believe that it is he and his firm who should be liable for attorney fees for this and any further hearings on this matter. My client is simply asking that Ms. O'Brian pay half the children's tuition. The cost to my client for the twelve hearings we have endured equate to an entire year of the children's tuition, and my client is adamant that this be the final hearing in this matter."

Again, #3 spoke up—and by the look of him, he knew he was under the gun. "Your Honor, my client is not here, and I cannot make this decision for her."

K was as assertive and forceful as I had ever seen him. "Your Honor, if we do not come to some conclusion today, I move that the child support be increased by $500 per month *and* that opposing counsel be held liable for all future charges incurred to litigate this matter."

I am usually very even keeled, but not on this day. My teeth were clenched, and I could feel my body vibrating as I held myself back from jumping up and screaming.

The judge looked over at me. I think she could tell I was ready to explode. She looked at the opposing counsel and said, "Mr. O'Brian's frustration with the system and the lack of progress here is completely understandable. I tend to agree. The request to simply split the tuition between the parents seems to be a reasonable request given that both Mr. and Ms. O'Brian have good and steady incomes. This hearing was scheduled over four weeks ago, and the fact that Ms. O'Brian did not take it seriously enough to attend should not be an excuse to take this any further. Ms. O'Brian is to pay to Mr. O'Brian one half the children's tuition in twelve installments on the first of each month beginning next month. If Ms. O'Brian wishes to contest this ruling, your brief must be filed within the next five business days. I suggest you properly explain things to your client. This shall conclude this matter, court adjourned."

The judge stood up, washing her hands of the ordeal. K, #3, and I stood up and in unison said, "Thank you, Your Honor."

After the judge walked out of the room, I fell back into my chair and tried to stop shaking. I put my head in my hands and sat motionless. After a few minutes, K brought me back to the moment, patted me on the shoulder, and said, "Let's go, Shane. We're done."

God promises to make something
good out of the storms that bring
devastation to your life.
—Romans 8:28

Chapter Eighteen
Takeaways and Action Items

- Remember to trust the professionals, but also remember to trust yourself.

- Anger is a potent emotion. It can be dangerous, but it can reveal problems clearly. Remember your strategies to stay calm, but listen to what your emotions are telling you.

CHAPTER NINETEEN

THE FINAL DIVORCE DECREE

I cannot celebrate while my children mourn.

When life is going well, time seems to pass at an ever-increasing speed. Before you know it, it's your birthday again, or Christmas, or the kids are getting out for summer break or going back to school . . . Everything seems to all happen in an instant.

When I was going through the darkest days of my divorce, it seemed as though time had stopped. The days were eternally long, and I felt that the next day or week would never come. It was hard to imagine that the divorce would ever actually be over. But the day did finally come, the day I signed the final paperwork, which granted the divorce and specified the terms and the reason for the divorce. The over two and a half years of hell . . . had seemed like ten.

In the end, the judge did see that the affair was obvious and therefore the grounds for the divorce were adultery and irreconcilable differences. The fact that the cause of the divorce was adultery gave the judge the power to split the assets up as he saw fit. I didn't get everything I asked for, but I got enough.

I was awarded the house and all the contents. I got to keep my home; and for my children's sake, that's what I wanted more than anything. I got my truck and Gigi got her van. Gigi got half of my retirement, which amounted to a couple thousand dollars, and I got half of her retirement, which was a very healthy sum that had accumulated over her twenty years of working for the airline.

I did not get the flight benefits I was asking for, and I was taken off the airline's health insurance program.

We had agreed to the fifty-fifty split of time with the kids, so that scenario remained the same. Gigi has them from the first through the fifteenth, and they're with me from the sixteenth through the end of the month.

One of the funny things I noticed in the divorce decree was that #3 was relieved of duty as Gigi's attorney. When I asked K about it, he told me that #3 had complained to him, saying that he would never again be the #2 lawyer for anyone, let alone #3. I don't think Gigi was his dream client.

When K called me to say it was finally done, it had been over six months since the trial had ended. After the trial, K had to submit a brief detailing our position on the divorce and the cause of the divorce. Then #3 had thirty days in which to respond to what K had written and write an opposing opinion for the judge. Both opinions cited case law to support their findings. All the back-and-forth took a few months, and the judge took almost three additional months to render his decision.

K was happy with himself; we had won. I had my house and everything in it, along with a substantial retirement account.

The final proposed settlement I had offered Gigi was a far better deal than what she got in the end. Had she decided to forego the trial, she would have retained all her retirement, and she could have taken any furnishings from the home she wanted. "You can lead a horse to water . . ."

The Final Divorce Decree

It's my understanding that narcissists will never compromise; and even in the face of certain loss, they'd prefer to give the responsibility of deciding their fate to a judge rather than making the decision themselves. If it's someone else making the call, they can always argue that the judge made a bad decision. It is never the narcissist's fault.

You would imagine that, at the end of something so terrible, your instinct would be to open a bottle of champagne and celebrate. I've heard of people actually having divorce parties celebrating the end of the marriage. It wasn't like that for me.

While I did feel relieved and happy that it was finally done, I didn't think celebrating was the right thing to do. I had always kept my kids in mind, and I knew that they were the big losers in all of it. It was their lives that were forever changed. It was the loss of their innocence; and this was something I knew I could never get back for them. Gigi and Jason made a decision to betray seven people: Jennifer, her two daughters, my three kids, and me. Would I have preferred that my marriage had never ended? While it truly was detrimental to my kids, I have to think that God, fate, or karma was looking at what Gigi and Jason truly held in their hearts, and it was decided that Jennifer and I didn't deserve to be treated in that way. So the short answer is that I'm glad Gigi is not my wife. She is not the person I thought she was, and she will never change.

The first person I told "the divorce is final" was Jennifer. She was very happy for me, and we toasted "to the end" over the phone. Jen's divorce from Jason took another eight months after mine was finalized; and at the time of this writing, they were still in court. Jason had agreed to their divorce and to a fifty-fifty split of his retirement account, but when it came time to sign the Qualified Domestic Relations Order, which is the paperwork necessary for the fund transfer, he refused. One other fun fact about narcissists? They don't pay their bills.

SHANE O'BRIAN

I went on to tell my friends and family members that things had been finalized and I was divorced. I thanked every one of them; for without them, I'm not sure I could have survived going through that deep valley and finally coming out the other side. No one I told about the end thought a celebration was in order. Everyone had a somber feeling toward the divorce. We were all relieved it was done, but we were cognizant of the fact that so many people had been hurt.

Life is an array of experiences, both good and bad. It's a journey, and hopefully when you overcome adversity, you'll have learned the most important lesson in life. By continuing on and never giving up, you live to see another day—and that day may be the most beautiful one ever. Realize that you are a much stronger person than you give yourself credit for.

Life is what you make of it, and no matter what fate or God has in store for you, face it with integrity and with a smile.

No one saves us but ourselves.
No one can and no one may.
We ourselves must walk the path.
—Buddha

Chapter Nineteen
Takeaways and Action Items

- If you feel like celebrating, then you should do that. It is natural and good to feel relieved and happy.

- If you don't feel like celebrating, then you shouldn't do that. It is also natural and fine to still grieve a deep loss.

- Whatever you feel at the final step of the legal process, that feeling is the right one for you. Resist letting others tell you how to feel.

CHAPTER TWENTY

FINDING PEACE

You'll never be happy until you accept your circumstance. Then it's just a matter of improving your lot in life.

It took years for me to finally accept what had happened to my children and me. The way things went down was surreal. It was reality; but for me, it seemed to be far worse than any fictional story even Stephen King could write.

Acceptance (Stage 5)

Acceptance didn't come in an instant. It wasn't something that I could nail down and say, "I am out!"

Instead, it was more of a slow realization and an eventual peaceful feeling that made me come to the conclusion I had indeed accepted this painful time in my life. I knew I was a changed person. I knew my children had been irreversibly hurt and their innocence had been taken from them at far too early an age. These are the facts, and to someone looking in from the outside it would seem obvious. Even so, I realize that you have to accept the shit that's thrown at you—and you have to move on. Some things are easy to say. But the doing? That's something altogether different.

How did I finally arrive at acceptance?

Self-reflection was a huge part of it. I had to consider my role in my marriage as well as my role in divorce. I'm proud of who I am and how I handled things. I'm proud of the way I faced adversity and took on a new role as mother and father. Because I took things on in an ethical manner—and I didn't give in to hate—I am able to look in the mirror and like the person looking back at me.

Therapy was a major factor in my eventual acceptance of my new reality. Having Dr. Faith's objective insight into everything that I was going through was a true blessing. She never told me what or how I should feel. Dr. Faith simply guided my thoughts so I could realize the facts that were staring me in the face. Sometimes when you are being pounded with evil, it's hard to see it and understand it until someone opens your eyes to it.

A continual effort to stay grounded was essential to my recovery and my acceptance of this life event. Reading and listening to a consistently positive message in books and in music kept me focused on the fact that life is great. It really is. Meditation helped me slow my mind so I could get through my day in one piece. Working out and physical activity gave my brain the respite needed to keep me going with a smile on my face.

The loss of my marriage was something that I accepted quickly; but in my humble opinion, a spouse is only one part of the puzzle. A family has many pieces. It was hard for me to accept the loss of the picture puzzle, the family. Without that one important piece, a husband or a wife, a mother or a father, the puzzle is no longer complete, and you have to go ahead and create a new picture without that one piece. This will happen in due course. It's not something that you can consciously do. It will naturally and gradually happen in its own time.

In my case, because Gigi initially made a concerted effort to stop her immediate family from helping me or having anything to do with me, the puzzle that was my family lost many more pieces than what

Finding Peace

was necessary. I'd been close to my in-laws, but that relationship soon became a casualty of the war my ex was waging. With that said, I'm sure the vast majority of the problem stemmed from Gigi's effort to isolate me and make my life as difficult as possible. This had such a terrible effect on my kids; and due to that fact, I was truly angry at my ex-in-laws. Everything and anything that was making my children suffer more was not acceptable to me. I told them so in no uncertain terms. Thankfully, things have changed since then.

For the most part, I'm back on speaking terms with Gigi's family. There were a lot of really bad things that transpired, and they were witnesses—and in many ways participants—in not only the mistreatment of me, but also that of my children. Do I consider them to be family members again? No, that won't happen. Am I angry with them for what they did? No, the anger with them has passed. They were thrown into a difficult situation with the rest of us, and Gigi is not a reasonable person, so on some level I get it.

I hope that, given the same circumstances, I would reject a call to abandon someone I care for. I hope I'd push back on the notion that I could not assist a soon-to-be-ex son-in-law or brother-in-law in the care of his children in their time of need.

Having a clear understanding of what happened and why it happened will go a long way in helping you to accept your new reality. The fact is that life is short—and you should take every day as a new day and make the very best of it. You're moving past the fork in your road. Be excited to see where your new path takes you. If you travel on it with a love of life and a dedication to be a positive influence in other people's lives, then you'll enjoy your journey on your new path, regardless of where it takes you.

A man cannot be comfortable without his own approval.
—Mark Twain

Chapter Twenty
Takeaways and Action Items

- The final stage of grief is acceptance, and acceptance brings freedom. Once you accept what has happened, you can move on.

- The journey to acceptance offers opportunities to make good choices and reflect on who you are as a man. You want to be able to look in the mirror at the end of the journey and like the man you have become.

- It is healthy to ask for help as you move toward acceptance. Therapy, self-reflection, and the other ways you keep yourself healthy are all important. I focused on media with positive messages, meditated, and stayed connected to friends and family in addition to exercise and therapy.

- Remember that losing your spouse is only one part of the loss you are experiencing. Take the time to understand and grieve the other losses as well.

- When you get to the end of the path of grief, take the time to be excited for where your new path might take you.

CHAPTER TWENTY-ONE

NEGOTIATING WITH K

If we all stopped looking away and fought for what we believe in and what we know is true, well, that would be a glorious day indeed.

After the dust settled, I set about the task of putting it all behind me and began to move forward again. I wanted to put a final stamp on everything and say goodbye to this part of my life. After the trial and child-support hearings were finally behind us, I still had a huge bill for K's services.

I'm not sure how most attorneys handle their billing, but K had always told me that he would re-evaluate my billing at the end and would adjust the fees if need be. It was a very ambiguous statement, but after all the utter bullshit I had endured over the two and a half years, I pushed him on it.

It was around this time that K ventured into representing criminal defendants, and he soon found himself in a high-profile murder trial. I was in no way concerned about K's workload or his issues, so I pushed him to lower my final bill. For the one month prior to and during the two-day trial, my bill totaled over $12,000, far exceeding the $10,000 he had estimated for the trial portion of the divorce. I repeatedly called his office to discuss the final bill with him, but he was always too busy. He handed me over to his sister, who was also in his firm, to negotiate a reduced billing.

SHANE O'BRIAN

I started dealing with K's sister, and I told her how things went down and the fact that K had done some things that were contrary to my instructions, not to mention the fact that he looked the other way when lawyers #2 and #3 failed to do their jobs as ordered by the court. While I didn't come right out and say I would take my argument to the ethics board, I did imply that, if needed, I would consider it. This was my kid's money, and I was not about to piss it away. During the time K was my lawyer, I tried to keep up with the charges each month; but toward the end, the tally was adding up faster than I could pay. The trial and the subsequent never-ending child support hearings all added into my final bill; it was almost $14,000. After a lot of negotiating, K's sister told me they would reduce the bill by half.

I meticulously went over all thirty-one itemized billing statements I had received from K's office. Looking at it made me ill. There were so many charges that were repeated over and over. It was things like calculating child support 11 times that drove up the charges.

After considering all the insanity and incessant back-and-forth between K. and Gigi's *three* lawyers, I told K's sister that I felt a larger discount was in order. I countered their offer with a final $5,000 payment, which could be paid over a one-year period.

They agreed.

I don't know if this will help you in your negotiations with your attorney, but be aware that to negotiate a final billing is common where I live.

My takeaway from all this is simple: Don't back down and do not let your attorney steal from you. This is your money and your future, so stand up to the system and let them know you're not stupid.

In business as in life,
You don't get what you deserve,
You get what you negotiate.
—Chester L. Karrass

Chapter Twenty-One

Takeaways and Action Items

- Remember to stand up for your rights—and your principles. You will want to know that you did the right thing at every step.

EPILOGUE

It took a couple years to come to the point that I could sit down and write this memoir. I knew I had a story to tell, a story that would give hope to the many people experiencing high-conflict divorce. I wanted to help *you* understand narcissism and push *you* to realize it is absolutely a real thing you simply cannot fight.

Gigi and Jason's relationship lasted far longer than Jennifer and I thought was possible, but after over five years together they split up. I still have friends in the airline industry, and they started to tell me how that relationship ended in flames, but I staved them off and said I would rather not know.

Jennifer is doing well. She is now happily married. She also finished her degree and is working as a social worker. She has a heart of gold. Unfortunately, over five years on, she is still fighting with Jason in court over child support.

My kids are doing well, as are Jennifer's. We did our best to keep them grounded, and I guess time will tell how everything works out for them.

Gigi and I do not co-parent our children, and I know Jennifer has the same issues with Jason. We both wish this aspect of life could be different but realize we do not have a choice in the matter.

I've given you only a small number of examples of the evil and malicious things Gigi and Jason leveled against the children, Jennifer, and me. It was truly difficult to watch the people I care for suffering at the hands of those two. I learned a long time ago that to hold onto that anger or hate that you feel, hurts only you. Be at peace with yourself and start living life again.

Dr. Wayne Dyer said it best. "No one ever died from a snake bite. Snakebites will never kill you. You can never be unbitten. It is not the bite that will kill you, but the venom that continues to pour through your system after the bite, that will end up destroying you." Don't let the venom from the bite of divorce kill you. Let it go and put it out of your system. If you have never read any of Dr. Dyer's books or haven't heard him speak, look him up and be inspired by a great mind.

As for me, I am still single and, in all likelihood, will remain so for the foreseeable future. It's not that I am opposed to the idea of falling in love again and settling down, it's just that God hasn't put that special person in my path yet. I am hopeful.

Thank you for joining me on my journey.

ACKNOWLEDGEMENTS

Making it through this time in my life took so many good and kind people it would be impossible to name them all. My brothers, sisters and mother were always there when I needed them. My children kept me grounded and gave me purpose.

Therapy sessions with Dr. Faith helped me to deal with the many issues my children were facing, and made me realize that life is full of change and how we handle and accept these changes can be the difference between joy and sorrow.

When I started this project, I had never been published and did not consider myself a writer. With the help of my writing coach Mary Deluca, I was able to organize my thoughts in a way that readers can understand. I am so grateful to Mountain Page Publishing for taking a chance on an unpublished author.

The hundreds of uplifting text messages, emails, and phone calls from Jennifer always gave me hope. More than anyone, thank you Jen. I am so happy you and your girls are well and happy.

www.ingramcontent.com/pod-product-compliance
Lightning Source LLC
Chambersburg PA
CBHW072010110526
44592CB00012B/1257